WS200   LAS

STK.
38-50
3616.

LHMC BOOK

54008000049237

Barts and The London
Queen Mary's School of Medicine and Dentistry

WHITECHAPEL LIBRARY, TURNER STREET, LONDON E1 2AD
020 7882 7110

4 WEEK LOAN
Books are to be returned on or before the last date below,
Otherwise fines may be charged

1 4 SEP 2009
02/10/09.

D1351372

Childhood Illness:
The Psychosomatic Approach

WILEY SERIES IN FAMILY PSYCHOLOGY

Series Editor

NEIL FRUDE
University of Wales College of Cardiff

Childhood Illness: The Psychosomatic Approach
Children Talking with Their Bodies
Bryan Lask and Abe Fosson

Further Titles in Preparation

Childhood Illness:
The Psychosomatic Approach

Children Talking with Their Bodies

Bryan Lask
Hospital for Sick Children
Great Ormond Street, London

and

Abe Fosson
University of Kentucky

John Wiley & Sons
Chichester · New York · Brisbane · Toronto · Singapore

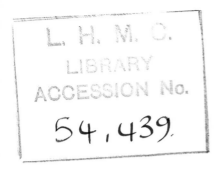

L. H. M. C.
LIBRARY
ACCESSION No.
54,439.

Copyright © 1989 by John Wiley & Sons Ltd.
Baffins Lane, Chichester,
West Sussex PO19 1UD, England

All rights reserved.

No part of this book may be reproduced by any means,
or transmitted, or translated into a machine language
without the written permission of the publisher.

Other Wiley Editorial Offices

John Wiley & Sons, Inc., 605 Third Avenue,
New York, NY 10158-0012, USA

Jacaranda Wiley Ltd, G.P.O. Box 859, Brisbane,
Queensland 4001, Australia

John Wiley & Sons (Canada) Ltd, 22 Worcester Road,
Rexdale, Ontario M9W 1L1, Canada

John Wiley & Sons (SEA) Pte Ltd, 37 Jalan Pemimpin # 05-04,
Block B, Union Industrial Building, Singapore 2057

British Library Cataloguing in Publication Data:

Lask, Bryan
    Childhood illness : the psychosomatic approach :
    children talking with their bodies.
    1. Children. Psychosomatic diseases. Therapy
    I. Title   II. Fosson, Abe
    618.92'008
    ISBN 0 471 91821 0
    ISBN 0 471 91822 9 pbk

Typeset by Acorn Bookwork, Salisbury, Wiltshire
Printed and bound in Great Britain by Biddles Ltd, Guildford, Surrey

This book is dedicated to our parents,
Aaron and Rita Lask,
and Abe and Tiny Fosson

Contents

Foreword

Occasionally a book is written at just the right time and place, and by the right people. This book is an outstanding example. At a time when doctors, not only in the western world but also internationally, are tending to specialize more in one organ and one age group, and to involve themselves in ever more detailed technological investigations, Dr Lask and Dr Fosson remind us of the need to assess the patient (the child) in the context of his family, his culture and neighbourhood, together with all environmental, educational and psychosocial influences. Too often, the paediatricians interested in such an holistic approach fail to relate satisfactorily with child psychiatrists and psychologists; and the child psychiatrists, who also are involved with such families, fail to speak at a level that is appropriate to the doctor who is responsible mainly for the child's physical welfare. The respective specialists then work within their own familiar territory and fail to communicate with others. The happiness and the value of this book is that it is written by a child psychiatrist and a paediatrician together and that, since each comes from a different country, their combined view has enhanced value. To me, it seems the child psychiatrist truly is a paediatrician's child psychiatrist, for he seems to understand the way paediatricians work and their level of knowledge. Similarly, the paediatrician has the characteristics of a child psychiatrist's paediatrician with the ability to explain the paediatric viewpoint to child psychiatrists and to work closely with them. It is a happy partnership.

Much of the book helps us to understand the many common pains, disorders and chronic symptoms of childhood, for which our pathological and radiodiagnostic tests reveal no answer. More importantly, the authors guide the clinician towards ways of helping the child. They do this in detail, beginning with general advice and leading on to specific examples of the techniques with which to interview the family, talk with the child and inaugurate practical and effective help. I am sure that this book will help to develop increased understanding between paediatricians and child psychiatrists but, more importantly, it provides a framework within which any doctor dealing with ill or unhappy children and troubled families can work, and will lead to better help for those children.

ROY MEADOW
Professor and Head of Department of Paediatrics and Child Health,
The University of Leeds

ix

Foreword

In this state-of-the-art volume a child psychiatrist and pediatrician with extensive experience in caring for sick children, in teaching about well and sick children, and in carrying out systematic clinical research on childhood enable us to hear more clearly 'children talking with their bodies.' Their perspective is stated clearly as they demonstrate the indivisibility of the body and mind. This integration is dramatized by the symptoms and findings of those psychosomatic illnesses that emphasize how health and illness states are represented more or less in both the body and the mind as our observational and technological capacities are able to detect, clarify and validate those states.

In this way, the interdependence of physical and psychosocial factors is clarified and illuminated, i.e., all illness, whatever its nature, must be considered from biological, developmental, psychological and social perspectives. When this process is the hall-mark of diagnostic, evaluative, therapeutic efforts the children not only talk with their bodies, but also enable us to infer what they are feeling, fearing, hoping, wishing and imagining, i.e., they also are enabled to talk with their minds and to minimize the isolation of physical from mental activities.

In this book the authors enable us to know that our knowledge base is a rapidly moving target because of our research momentum, and that it is increasingly essential to keep up with this momentum by conceptualizations that are designed to have room for the newest findings of epidemiology, human genetics, molecular biology, biochemistry, the neural sciences and developmental psychology, while enlarging and refining the usefulness of psychodynamic methods and formulations.

By starting with empirical findings at the surface – e.g., symptoms of pain, nausea, emotional distress, pruritus, diarrhea, etc, – and moving toward the systems in which these findings are manifest, the authors demonstrate repeatedly that there is an ever-changing hierarchy of body and mind involvement as one comes into a diagnostic–therapeutic relationship with differing disorders. Thus, asthma is different from an infectious disease, though they both involve body and mind at differing levels of causation and expression.

Similarly, the authors have demonstrated the social ecological hierarchy of child, family and community. These are the contexts in which the illness states take place, find expression and have their meaning defined and weighted by a specific culture and by particular historical epochs.

This prepares the reader for a very similar approach to treatment through the child, the family and the neighborhood or community. These concepts bring into view a working awareness of the common pathways of sickness expression, leaving room for the assessment and treatment of morphological deficits, physiological maladaptive responses and psychosocial reinforcements.

This enables us to avoid artificial classifications of sickness states and will insure a systematic process of relating the various aspects of illness experiences. Thus, the authors provide a scaffold for such a process when they speak of predisposing, precipitating, perpetuating, and protective factors common to all conditions of illness.

By developing this focus on the psychosomatic disorders of childhood and adolescence – e.g., asthma, diarrhea, failure-to-thrive, recurrent febrile sore throats, headaches, anorexia nervosa and bulimia – the authors take into account in a balanced way how the child's physician gauges the severity of illness in the context of the child's developmental capacities and deviations; and how the physician becomes increasingly aware of the child's responses to noxious as well as normative physical and psychological challenges. For example, just as they pair stress and immune responses, the authors also provide useful pointers about how to integrate into the diagnosis and treatment of each child the awareness that pains, stresses and illnesses are experienced uniquely by the growing, developing child who is required to adapt socially as well as biologically.

This small, basic book is able to convey at a richly conceptual level, implicitly as well as explicitly, how thoughtful diagnosis and evaluation promote the psychotherapeutic role of those who are providing health care for the child and guidance for the parents. Such clinical experiences carried on in systematic research with epidemiological dimensions can become the basis for social and health policies for a community and a nation. Throughout, the authors create an intellectual climate that fosters collaboration across the various disciplines involved. They never lose sight of the necessity for continuity of care and a therapeutic alliance between child, parents and the physician or therapist of record.

June 30, 1989   ALBERT J. SOLNIT, M.D.
                                                          Yale University, New Haven CT

Series Preface

A common definition of the term 'psychology' is 'the study of human experience and behaviour'. Since everybody strives to understand people there is a sense in which we are all psychologists. Certainly those in the 'helping professions' (medicine, nursing, social work, physiotherapy, dentistry, etc.) as well as those in many other professions (teaching, managing, advertising) are in their everyday work applying their understanding of human beings and their relationships. The degree to which they are effective as professionals will depend largely on the accuracy of their understanding.

Traditionally, psychology as an academic discipline focused on subsystems such as the visual system, or on phenomena such as learning. In many cases the phenomena were studied in the 'pure' environment of the psychological laboratory, with extraneous noises and influences ('reality') excluded as far as possible. In recent years, however, much has changed. Increasingly there has been a concern to integrate knowledge about different systems and different phenomena. The individual has been examined in a more 'holistic' fashion. Concepts such as 'mind', 'self' and 'person' have become respectable. The person has been acknowledged to be an agent, actively choosing between alternatives rather than being 'forced' by circumstances to behave in one way or another. There has been an increasing concern that the phenomena studied in experimental settings should be relevant to how people actually behave in the real world. Studies are now judged partly by their 'ecological validity'. 'Human ethology' concerns how people behave in their 'normal habitat', which is now acknowledged to include homes, restaurants, theatres and the workplace.

In days not long past it was difficult to find any reference to 'the family' in textbooks of psychology. Even in textbooks on 'social psychology' there was scant mention of social relationships between intimates. There was a lot on eye contact between strangers, a lot on communication within 'committee' or 'jury' groups, and a lot on prejudice against minority groups. Psychologists' own apparent prejudice against studying long-term and intimate relationships—those that most matter to the individual—passed for the most part without acknowledgement. Even today 'family psychology' is not a major part of the undergraduate psychology curriculum. It seems that this is likely to change, however, for there has recently been a great deal of research into long-term relationships, and many relevant books and journals are beginning to emerge.

Psychologists have increasingly come to accept that understanding people often implicates understanding the relationships they are involved in, that it is important to understand 'the spaces between individuals', and that familiies are complex systems that demand new forms of analysis.

There has always been a much greater appreciation of the importance of family factors in certain of the disciplines that lie adjacent to psychology—in particular, sociology, anthropology and psychiatry. These have contributed a rich literature on family psychology for many years. This is now being further enriched by the work of many psychologists.

The extreme importance of these studies for a wide range of professions has prompted the Wiley Series in Family Psychology. Too often, material from research and clinical studies is widely scattered across journals relating to many different disciplines, so that few professionals are able to become familiar with and integrate information sufficiently well to form an up-to-date view of any particular field within the family psychology area. Contributors to the series are specialists who have been invited to provide such an integration for a wide professional readership. The fact that not all of the authors in the series are psychologists by profession reflects the fact that many other professionals know a great deal about family psychology.

In the present volume, a child psychiatrist and a paediatrician, both with wide clinical and research experience, present a current view on childhood illness. The authors demonstrate the interaction between biological, psychological and social factors, and show that a multifactorial approach is essential for accurate diagnosis and treatment. Following from this analysis, emphasis is placed on interdisciplinary teamwork. Physicians, nurses, psychologists and other pro-fessionals who deal with families in which a child presents with a somatic complaint will learn a great deal from their analysis. Lask and Fosson have an approach which is humane, warm, sensitive and practical, and they write with a light touch. They illustrate their text with numerous clinical examples and pass on many tips and techniques that have evolved during the course of their clinical experience. Many of these will prove of immediate use to professionals from many disciplines. They review a broad spectrum of therapeutic approaches, emphasizing that the wider the range of possible treatments considered the more likely professionals are to be able to help.

NEIL FRUDE

Acknowledgements

First and foremost we wish to thank Judith and Sue for their invaluable and unfailing support, advice and encouragement, and Judith also for her immense hard work, good humour, and tolerance in preparing innumerable drafts and the final manuscript.

We are grateful to Neil Frude for his most helpful comments, Bob Herndon for his illustrations, and Nancye Louderback for her assistance at all stages. We are indebted beyond measure to our patients and their families for both tolerating and teaching us so much.

Last, but definitely not least, we wish to acknowledge how much we have learned over the years from our many colleagues, and most particularly our mentors, Otto Wolff, John Apley, and Warren Wheeler.

Prologue

The psychosomatic approach is listening to the child talking with his body (Anon.)

This is a book for those who would like to understand and deal with children's illness in both its physical and emotional context. At its broadest it is about all children, for without exception all children are ill from time to time. Traditional medical practice has determined that physical symptoms mean physical ill health, yet in the majority of instances such symptoms are a response to stress, a signal of distress. This book is about the integration of what for thousands of years (with some honourable exceptions) have been falsely separated—the physical and the psychological. The anonymous aphorism 'listening to the child talking with his body' summarizes our philosophy far better than we could.

Our intention throughout is that of integration. We attempt to integrate body and mind; paediatrics and psychological medicine; the work of physicians and non-physicians; children and their environment; varying and sometimes contrasting theoretical models; and the many different schools of therapy. We even attempt to integrate views from both sides of the Atlantic, at times a more difficult task than integrating the psyche and soma. However, given the impossibility of integrating the vastly different ways in which our common language is spoken and spelt, we have given up on that task, and settled for the senior version! And whilst on style, we want to make clear that we have every respect for anti-sexist policy, but none whatsoever for the use of 'he/she' or 's(he)'. Because we are in general discussing our ideas and our work we have tended to use 'he' or 'him' as a generic pronoun, although occasionally the tedious 'he or she' has slipped in.

The book starts in Chapter 1 with a search for meaning of the many different terms and euphemisms that so often serve only to confuse. We hope that we have achieved some clarification of such concepts as psychosomatic illness, somatization and somatization disorders, psychosomatic approach, comprehensive approach, and linear and circular causality. We have included a detailed model for understanding contributory factors to physical symptoms, which attempts to integrate the biological, social and psychological components. In Chapter 2 we explain, in what we hope is a clear way, the complex psycho-

xvii

physiological pathways that determine the conversion of stress and distress into physical symptoms. Chapter 3 contains a compendium of the many different physical symptoms and clinical features. Each major group and their subgroups are described in detail, with reference to cause, incidence, distribution and prognosis. Any specific treatment is also mentioned, but fuller details of treatment are provided later in the book. Chapter 4 describes the illness network, all that happens in and around the child, his illness, the family and the outside world. An integrated approach to assessment with attention focused on physical, social and psychological components is described in Chapter 5.

The second half of the book focuses on treatment. Chapter 6 introduces an integrated approach to treatment, including description of how best to involve children and parents to ensure successful outcome, and discussion of liaison between colleagues and differentiation of professional roles. In Chapter 7 we focus on working with parents, including the application of behaviour therapy, and Chapter 8 contains an overview of family therapy. Individual therapies are described in Chapter 9, and pharmacological treatments for somatization in Chapter 10.

Each chapter is prefaced by a light-hearted and undemanding guide to the reader. We hope that these will encourage a perusal or even a more detailed study of the contents. It is not essential to read each chapter in sequence, for each has relevance in its own right. Just as in John Donne's words 'no man is an island, entire of itself; every man is a continent, a part of the main' (*Meditation xviii*) so each section of the book deals with some aspect of the child's world, and each aspect contributes to an understanding of the whole child.

CHAPTER 1

A Search for Meaning

This is the great error of our day, that physicians separate the mind from the body (Plato, 320 BC)

GUIDE FOR THE READER

In this chapter we heed Plato's warning and try to make sense of many conceptual and semantic confusions which, even 2300 years later, have led to his advice being all too frequently ignored. We then discuss the psychosomatic approach and the role of predisposing, precipitating, perpetuating and protective factors in childhood disorder.

1.1 INTRODUCTION

Much confusion occurs about the meaning of such terms as 'psychosomatic', 'psychogenic', 'psychosocial' and 'somatization', and this is compounded by the inconsistency that exists between professionals, whereby some emphasize the physical component, others the psychosocial. We need careful definitions of commonly used terms and concepts to overcome this confusion.

1.2 DEFINITIONS AND CONCEPTUALIZATIONS

The term 'psychosomatic' was first used in 1818 by the German psychiatrist Heinioth when describing the origin of insomnia (Margetts, 1950), and has since been used (and abused) to convey so many different ideas that it is in danger of losing its value. If it is to be used at all then it should be to mean the inseparability and interdependence of psychosocial and biological aspects of humankind (Lipowski, 1984, p. 83).

'Psychogenic' means quite simply having psychological origin, and 'psycho-social' refers to the interdependence of psychological and social factors.

The term 'psychosomatic disorder' was first used to draw attention to the fact that psychological factors play a part in many physical disorders, such as

1

asthma, peptic ulcer, thyrotoxicosis and rheumatoid arthritis (Alexander, 1950). However, implicit in such terminology is the existence of 'non-psychosomatic disorders' i.e. disorders in which psychological factors are irrelevant. This simplistic view is now clearly untenable, but many are still unable to accept Lipowski's statement (1974) that all diseases physical and mental are multi-factorial in origin.

Unfortunately the medical profession is slow to learn, and despite Plato's admonition medical practice is bedevilled by the tendency (or in some cases the determination) to think in terms of 'either/or'. Either the disease is organic, in which case psychological factors are insignificant, or there is an obvious psycho-logical problem so organic factors can be discounted. Even many mental health professionals subscribe to this simplistic view by sometimes offering psycholog-ical interpretations of physical illness, or taking an exclusively medical or biological approach to psychiatric disorder. Such views unfortunately also inform, or rather misinform, the treatment process.

We believe that it is more logical and sensible to think in terms of a continuum of illness or disorder, from predominantly organic aetiology on the one hand, to predominantly psychosocial aetiology on the other (Figure 1.1). Such a view allows the appropriate emphasis, but does not exclude the possibil-ity (and in some instances the probability) of additional aetiological factors.

Figure 1.1 Spectrum of aetiology

For example, an indisputably structural disorder such as congenital heart disease would be placed at the organic end of the spectrum (position 1), whilst a purely behavioural problem such as school phobia would be at the other extreme (position 7). However, school phobia presenting with abdominal pain may be slightly nearer to the centre (position 5), for presumably there is an underlying physiological substrate that determines abdominal pain to be the presenting symptom. Recurrent respiratory tract infections might be placed at position 3 for, although there is undoubtedly an organic (bacterial or viral) origin, poor social circumstances or high levels of stress predispose the child to infection. Anorexia nervosa might be placed at position 6 given its primarily psychological origins, but the self-starvation produces aetiologically relevant biological se-quelae. Diabetes mellitus may be in any position from 1 to 9 given the possibility of stress in its origins, and the importance of psychosocial factors in its control. The possibilities and permutations are endless, and differ also over time. What initiates an illness process may not be what keeps it going.

Another term that creates confusion is 'somatization'. Lipowski (1967) again offers the most useful definition: 'The tendency to experience, conceptualize and/or communicate psychological states or contents as bodily sensations, functional changes, or somatic metaphors'. In other words somatization is that process whereby distress is experienced and/or expressed in somatic or physical terms. The simplest and most common manifestations are, in adults, tension headaches, and, in children, 'bellyaches'. In more complex forms somatization may present as virtually any physical symptom or contribute to any physical disorder (see Chapters 3 and 4). In adults, for example, peptic ulcers, ischaemic heart disease and hypertension (raised blood pressure) may all represent the end-point of a somatization process. In childhood, failure to thrive, gastrointestinal disease and seizure disorders may be manifestations of the same process.

Many psychiatrists have made determined attempts to categorize the myriad forms of somatized distress. For example, somatization phenomena have been classified on a psychopathological basis (Lipowski, 1967) as follows:

(1) physical concomitants of depression
(2) physiological concomitants of anxiety
(3) hysterical conversion phenomena
(4) manifestations of hypochondriasis
(5) somatosensory hallucinations and delusions
(6) manifestations of classical 'psychosomatic' disorders such as hypertension or peptic ulcer
(7) communication of distress in bodily language

More recently, and in contrast, Kirmayer (1986) has pointed out that the term is used in at least four different clinical situations:

(1) a style of symptom presentation
(2) a tendency to attribute problems to somatic causes
(3) a distinct psychiatric disorder
(4) a presumed aetiology for functional somatic symptoms

Both Lipowski and Kirmayer acknowledge that there is overlap between classification, with no sharp demarcation. It is of interest that for over twenty years attempts have been made to categorize somatization phenomena, but with no universally acceptable schema. It seems obvious now that the determined attempts of psychiatrists to categorize the myriad forms of expression of human distress have done little to further our understanding of somatization, and have tended rather to confuse. It seems more important to understand the origins of a child's distress, why he or she somatizes that distress, what perpetuates it, and which treatment is most useful, than to determine into which diagnostic subcategory the problem most neatly fits.

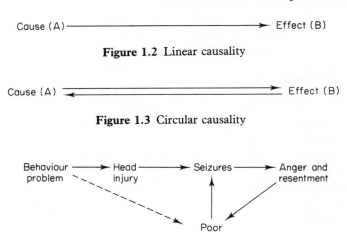

Figure 1.2 Linear causality

Figure 1.3 Circular causality

Figure 1.4 An example of circular causality

So we shall use the term 'somatization' to mean the physical experience and/or expression of human distress. The anonymous quotation at the head of our Prologue leads to an almost perfect definition—somatization is the child talking with his body.

Two other concepts that are relevant to this discussion are 'linear causality' and 'circular causality'. The former refers to the traditional understanding of aetiology in which a cause (A) has an effect (B). (See Figure 1.2.) For example, an asthma attack leads to anxiety, or an infection causes pneumonia. The reader will already have predicted our criticism of this simplistic perspective. The reality is far more complex, but at its simplest is conveyed in Figure 1.3. The anxiety caused by the asthma attack has the potential of maintaining the episode or triggering a further attack at a later date. This two-way interaction between cause and effect is known as 'circular causality'. Needless to say, it can be far more complex, and it is discussed in more detail in Chapter 4. For the moment we need not be surprised by sequences such as that conveyed by Figure 1.4 showing how a behaviour-disordered 13-year-old boy who stole and crashed a motor bike ends up with a poorly controlled seizure disorder. Only a model of circular causality can convey the complexities of this process

1.3 THE PSYCHOSOMATIC APPROACH

In practice virtually all disorders have multifactorial causation—multicausality is the rule, not the exception (Kirmayer, 1986). The multiple factors to be considered include developmental, biological (organic), social and psychological.

Recent research has made it clear that the risk of becoming seriously ill is affected more profoundly by social factors than by physical wear and tear (Totman, 1979).

An excellent example in adult medicine of the intimate relationship between all these factors is that of coronary artery disease. Consider, for example, a type A personality (Friedman, 1969)—a middle-aged male, experiencing considerable stress in his demanding but predominantly sedentary occupation, who comes from a family with a history of coronary thrombosis. He tends to smoke to calm his nerves, and works ever harder to stem the tide. He is too busy to take time off, relax or even have the occasional medical check, when he might have discovered that his blood pressure was raised. He is too tired and irritable to respond positively to the needs and demands of his wife and teenage children, who openly express their resentment at his unavailability. He is additionally worried by the increasing frequency of one of the children's asthma attacks and concerned at the other's rebellious (teenage) behaviour. A multitude of factors have contributed to his inevitable heart attack:

(1) developmental—peak risk age group
(2) biological—genetic, sedentary occupation, no exercise and raised blood pressure
(3) psychological—type A personality, high level of anxiety and poor coping skills
(4) social—overwhelming job demands
(5) family—unresolved conflicts and resentment, and ill health

In Chapter 4 we consider the way in which possible reactions to such an event can perpetuate the problem. But let us now consider a similar scenario in childhood.

Adrian, aged 11, has developed a persistent, unremitting dry cough, about six weeks after changing schools. Detailed physical examination and investigation reveal no organic cause, but his general condition is deteriorating. He has no appetite, has lost 5 kg and is feeling exhausted. He can no longer cope with going to school, and he is obviously depressed. Referral for psychiatric assessment reveals the following background. His parents separated two years previously but remain fairly friendly. His father has a new partner and Adrian stays with them alternate weekends. He feels guilty because he knows that his mother is lonely, having recently ended a brief and violent relationship. One year previously she was found to have a malignant tumour, for which she had refused surgery, but had accepted radiotherapy. She did not want to be followed up and refused to discuss this with anyone. Adrian had been relatively healthy until recently, apart from recurrent upper respiratory infections, and a period of separation anxiety when he first started school.

Once again we can see how multiple factors interact to produce a major physical problem:

(1) developmental—age of transition from small, friendly primary school to large secondary school
(2) biological—vulnerability to upper respiratory infections predisposes Adrian to recurrent coughing
(3) psychological—sensitive and anxious child with an earlier history of separation difficulty
(4) social—difficulty settling in new school, making friends and coping with a less friendly school environment
(5) family—Adrian has to cope with divided loyalties, wanting to be with both of his separated parents; and the absence of communication about his mother's potentially fatal illness exacerbates pre-existing concerns

Such a combination of factors must almost inevitably lead to a stress reaction. The psychogenic cough is the obvious one, given his previous medical history (see also Chapter 3). The psychophysiological processes involved are considered in more detail in Chapter 2.

Another method of exploring the multifactorial contributions to a disorder is by using the '3 Ps': (1) predisposing, (2) precipitating and (3) perpetuating factors. In Adrian's case the *predisposing* factors were his biological vulnerability to upper respiratory tract infections, his anxiety about separation, exacerbated by his parents' separation, and the possibility of his mother's death; the *precipitating* factor was the change of school; the *perpetuating* factors included his divided loyalties, and the blocked communication, so that he was unable to discuss openly his distress.

In the remainder of this chapter we need to consider in detail what predisposes children to somatize, and what are the most common predisposing, precipitating and perpetuating factors. We also discuss later a fourth 'P'— 'protective factors'.

1.4 PREDISPOSING FACTORS

There are many potential predisposing factors, and for any particular child it is probable that a combination is involved.

1.4.1 Biological vulnerability (or substrate)

Most people have vulnerable organs or systems that become targetted. For example, children with asthma have bronchial hyperreactivity—a breathing tube which is hypersensitive to stimuli and therefore readily goes into spasm. The predisposition to hyperreactivity appears to be inherited, whilst environmental factors are required for the asthma to be manifested (Gregg, 1983). What distinguishes the asthmatic child from the normal child is the predisposition to bronchial hyperreactivity. So stress factors may precipitate an asthma attack, but cannot cause asthma. Nor does asthma have symbolic meaning, despite determined statements to that effect in the psychosomatic literature. This concept of illness having a symbolic meaning is critically discussed elsewhere (Lask, 1987b).

Any part or system of the body may be physiologically vulnerable and therefore become the biological substrate. Common examples besides asthma include migraine, peptic ulcer, urticaria and juvenile arthritis. This process is more fully described in Chapter 2. In chronic diseases, such as cystic fibrosis or diabetes, which are persistent rather than recurrent, stress factors may directly exacerbate the problem so that, for example, the diabetic has more difficulty maintaining satisfactory blood sugar levels, and becomes more liable to episodes of hypo- or hyperglycaemia. The child with cystic fibrosis may find that breathing becomes even more difficult.

The mechanisms are 'direct' in that stress is the precipitant of a psychophysiological process, the end-point being an exacerbation or intensification of the illness. Stress can also influence the disorder in a less direct way by influencing the child's behaviour and self-care (see Chapter 4).

1.4.2 Physiological responses to stress

Stress produces a number of physiological reactions regardless of underlying biological vulnerabilities. For example, when anxious we all have normal autonomic responses such as increased pulse rate, palpitations, restlessness and sweating. Some may experience breathlessness, nausea or frequency of micturition. Frequently children may focus specifically on one or more such responses, reporting or demonstrating the *response* to the anxiety, rather than the *anxiety* itself. For example, muscle tensions may be perceived and reported as pain (see Chapter 2).

1.4.3 Early life experiences

These are important predisposing factors for illness, especially when there has been a history of childhood exposure to illness, or of parental over-concern with bodily functions (Engel, 1968). Children may identify with symptomatic parents and model their illness behaviour; or produce at a later time symptoms that had previously led to parental concern.

1.4.4 Personality characteristics

These have been linked with the tendency to somatize, although there is no clear agreement concerning predisposing personality traits. It seems likely that some individuals have a reduced capacity to conceptualize and express emotion. Sifneos (1973) has coined the term 'alexithymia' to describe the state of being unable to express emotions in words. It is probable that any such children would come from families in whom emotional expression is inhibited, and there is a tendency to somatize as a means of communicating distress.

There is no evidence for the frequently stated view that specific disorders correlate with specific personality characteristics or attitudes (e.g., Graham, 1972). We agree with Grolnick (1972), who states that it is fallacious to assume a linear correlation between events at the levels of physiological and psychological integration.

1.4.5 Sociocultural influences

In most societies physical ill health is far more acceptable than psychological problems or illness. Physical symptoms are perceived as beyond the individual's control, whereas psychiatric symptomatology, such as anxiety or depression, is still stigmatized as weakness, madness or self-induced, and so not worthy of sympathy or attention. An undue focus on somatic symptoms is understandable in such a context. In addition, sociocultural factors can determine whether a particular individual may experience a specific form of illness (McHugh and Vallis, 1986, p. 19), and whether an individual will seek help or adopt a more resigned approach (Leigh and Reiser, 1980, p. 6).

Fads and fashions also contribute to the somatization process. The current preoccupation with health, beauty and fitness has led to an intense preoccupation with body size and appearance. Reduction of food intake to control body weight is endemic in teenage girls, of whom an increasing number are developing anorexia nervosa (see Chapter 3). Physicians are also responsive to fashion and are prone to make fashionable diagnoses such as food allergy or myalgic encephalopathy (ME) (see Chapter 3) with minimal evidence. Once more, such labelling may only serve to reinforce the problem.

1.5 PRECIPITATING FACTORS

Inseparable from the idea of precipitating factors is the concept of '*stress*', one of those frequently used terms that defies a universally acceptable definition. In its simplest psychological sense, stress is any stimulus sufficiently intense to produce an unpleasant emotional response. The '*stress reaction*' is the individual's biochemical, physiological or psychological response to stress—in a word, '*distress*'.

Whether a specific stressor does indeed create distress will be dependent upon the individual's personal history and biological and psychological dispositions, so that what is stress for one person may not be for another. Attempts have been made to devise life-event scales (Holmes and Rahe, 1967) which purport to measure the number of stressors for any individual, and modifications of these have been prepared for children (e.g., Monaghan *et al.*, 1979). However, it has been pointed out that the qualitative and quantitative values assigned by children often differ from those of adult professionals who devise the scales (Yeaworth *et al.*, 1980) and the validity of such scales remains suspect.

Notwithstanding the variation between individuals there are certain universal stressors (Garmezy and Rutter, 1985; Rutter and Cox, 1985). These tend to fall into two major categories: infrequent but major life events, and frequent daily hassles. They include: (1) the disruption of attachment relationships (loss); (2) persistent rejection or lack of affection, or persisting neglect or abuse; (3) parental ill health including mental illness; (4) chronically disturbed family relationships such as marital or parental discord, generational skewing, i.e. inappropriate over-involvement of a parent and child, or distorted or deviant communication patterns; (5) life events or changes which require important, and potentially difficult, social adaptations, such as birth of a sibling, change of school or impending examinations; and (6) major traumas such as serious accidents, assault, illness or injury, parental unemployment or homelessness.

A recent cross-cultural study indicated that children from six different cultures were broadly in agreement with regard to what were the potentially most stressful events. Of 20 undesirable life-events the top five were losing a parent, going blind, academic failure, wetting in class and potential fights (Yamamoto *et al.*, 1987).

The evidence for the association of such stressors with somatic responses is considerable. Garmezy and Rutter (1985, p. 155) have noted an association between stressful events and rheumatoid arthritis, malignancy, ulcerative colitis, peptic ulcer, rheumatic fever, neurodermatitis, hepatitis, diabetes, respiratory tract illnesses, chronic illness, hospitalization, high injury rates and accidents. Even pyloric stenosis in infancy has been correlated with high levels of maternal stress in the third trimester of pregnancy.

1.6 PERPETUATING FACTORS

1.6.1 The overlap

What precipitates distress may well also perpetuate it. If, for example, a child is teased by peers to the point he feels sick, the nausea may well persist for as long as the teasing. Thus the teasing both precipitates and perpetuates the problem (in a predisposed child). Equally, however, the teasing may have long ceased, but the nausea has persisted for other reasons. There is therefore an important distinction between the precipitating and perpetuating factors. Frequently it is possible to identify an initial precipitant which has long since ceased, and bewilderment accompanies the persisting symptoms. Conversely, it may be clear that the symptoms have predated an obvious current stress, and the original cause is lost in the mists of time.

In the rest of this section we consider factors additional to those discussed under precipitants that may perpetuate a problem.

1.6.2 Primary and secondary gain

Primary gain is the relief of anxiety by symptom production. *Secondary gain* is the benefit obtained from the symptoms, usually the avoidance of unpleasant situations. Consider, for example, an 11-year-old child fearful of school. The onset of abdominal pain draws attention away from the anxiety and focuses it instead on the pain—primary gain. If the pain also leads to days off school then the feared situation is avoided—secondary gain. As both consequences have an element of 'reward', either may be rewarding and thus serve to maintain the symptom.

1.6.3 Reinforcement

Somatization may be reinforced by those around the child, so setting up a self-perpetuating process. For example, a parent may not respond when a child is seeking attention in a direct way, but anxiously attend to physical symptoms. The child, now getting the attention required, experiences further symptoms which eventually lead to a request for medical advice. At this point physicians may reinforce the problem, either by failing to recognize the process and initiating unnecessary investigations, or by 'medicalizing' it by giving it a medical diagnosis, such as spastic colon or periodic syndrome (see Chapter 3).

1.6.4 Disposition

While some children tend to be stoical in the face of physical symptoms, others become anxious, panicky and overwhelmed. This heightened emotional arousal exacerbates and intensifies the symptoms and contributes to a vicious cycle of ill health and anxiety.

1.6.5 Sociocultural influences

In the same way as sociocultural factors may predispose children to illness, so also may they perpetuate the problem. In a society where stress is denied, or distress is seen as weakness, physical explanations for physical symptoms will be tenaciously sought, and psychological exploration will not be considered. The symptoms are inevitably perpetuated by this process.

1.6.6 Family influences

A similar point applies to families. Some families either deny that their child is under stress or refuse to accept that stress can produce physical symptoms. The determined refusal to acknowledge, accept and therefore handle appropriately the child's distress leaves the child no option but to continue showing the symptoms. The family denial perpetuates the problem.

Family discord, generational skewing, over-protectiveness and parental ill health all previously mentioned as stress factors, can of course also perpetuate symptoms (see also Chapter 8).

1.7 PROTECTIVE FACTORS

Insufficient is known about factors that protect children exposed to stress. As with so much else it is likely that a complex of characteristics determine whether a child succumbs to adversity. Garmezy (1984) has reviewed this topic in depth, and concludes that key factors include such temperamental attributes as activity level, social responsiveness and adaptability. Others agree with Garmezy that familial and communal social supports are very important. A good harmonious relationship with one parent (Rutter and Cox, 1985) and a good sibship (Wallerstein, 1983) and other sources of self-esteem (e.g., success at school) aid successful adaptation to stress.

On a lighter but just as important note Apley has introduced the concept of emotional vitamins (1982) for a child's healthy development. These include: (1) a good relationship with at least one parent ('you are loved'); (2) good supervision ('you are secure'); (3) respect as an individual ('you are you'); (4) encouragement and recognition of effort and achievement ('you matter'); and (5) gradually increasing responsibility and social involvement ('you are growing up').

1.8 SUMMARY

(1) 'Psychosomatic' refers to the interdependence of physical and psychosocial factors.
(2) 'Somatization' is that process whereby distress is experienced or expressed in somatic (or physical) terms.
(3) There are no 'psychosomatic disorders' as such, any more than there are 'non-psychosomatic disorders'. All illness, whatever its nature, needs to be

considered from biological, developmental, psychological and social perspectives, i.e. the psychosomatic approach.

(4) A helpful way of considering the multifactorial contribution to disorders is to subdivide these into predisposing, precipitating and perpetrating factors.

(5) 'Predisposing' factors include physiological vulnerability, early life experiences, behavioural and physiological responses to stress, sociocultural and family influences.

(6) 'Precipitating' factors include any events that stress the child. 'Stress' is any stimulus sufficiently intense to produce an unpleasant emotional response—'distress'.

(7) 'Perpetuating' factors include any persisting stressors, temperamental predisposition to anxiety, the relief from stress due to somatization, reinforcement by significant others such as parents, teachers or doctors, and denial of the child's emotional distress.

(8) Factors that protect children from somatization include temperamental attributes such as adaptability, a good relationship with at least one parent, a strong supportive sibship and good communal support.

In the next chapter we describe the mechanisms involved in psychophysiological processes.

CHAPTER 2

Psychophysiological Mechanisms

People are precariously adjusted machines, walking bags of intestines, boxes of telephone nerves, chemical factories liable to go wrong at any minute . . . (Olaf Stapeldon, 1932)

GUIDE FOR THE READER

This chapter deals with the connections between emotional arousal and physiological responses. Knowledge in this area is very useful when faced with the patient's or family's cognitive rejoinders, and it is important to be able to explain such mechanisms in simple terms. Explanations of physiological mechanisms are given for individuals not well versed in human pathophysiology.

2.1 INTRODUCTION

As it becomes clearer that all disease processes are influenced by psychosocial stressors and that, reciprocally, the psychological state of all patients is influenced by their disease, it has become obvious that most illnesses have multiple contributing factors (not one patient, one disease, one cause, as has been the traditional concept in medicine). The relative influence of psychosocial factors on the diverse aspects of illness is considerable. An exception is the determination of the site of pathology, which seems to be entirely biological. There is no basis for the commonly held opinions that the site of pathology, or type of symptom, is 'chosen' by the patient, or determined by psychological factors such as 'symbolic meaning'.

Four basic mechanisms and their various clinical permutations are understood sufficiently to warrant discussion. These are: (1) the physiology, perception and communication of pain; (2) biological vulnerability; (3) stress and the autonomic nervous system; and (4) host defences and the interactions of stress with the immune response.

13

2.2 PAIN

The interpretation of stimuli is not as simple as 'it either hurts or it doesn't', or even 'it's organic or non-organic pain'.

Pain is both an internal signal to the brain from various peripheral sites and an external communication from the suffering individual to others. Both these private and public aspects of pain are complexly related and responsive to cognitive and psychosocial variables. The internal aspects of pain are limited by the physical and functional aspects of the nervous system, but within these limits major variations are determined by psychosocial factors. The external communication of pain is age-dependent and even more responsive to environmental factors.

Understanding physiological aspects of pain is necessary for dealing with childhood chronic pain syndromes. Communication within the nervous system is binary, with the central nervous system either receiving an impulse (+), or not receiving an input (−), from afferent (input) neurones innervating various body tissues. Impulses are constantly arriving to the brain from the skin and extremities, so that the individual can be consciously aware of the sensation from these areas. The ability to receive similar information from within the head, chest and abdomen is relatively limited. Consequently, in processing sensations from internal sites, there is considerable limitation of one's ability to discriminate between noxious stimuli of different intensities, and to report accurately a particular experience as painful. This, combined with the inability to evaluate by direct observation the anatomical structures in question, when complaints emanate from internal compartments, explains why childhood chronic pain syndromes predominantly involve the head, chest and abdomen.

Physiologically pain is not an 'all-or-nothing' phenomenon, but a central interpretation of neuronal impulses. Vast numbers of incoming impulses are evaluated at a preconscious level, and ignored or acted upon, without reaching conscious awareness. Specific neurones always carry the same type of information, for example hot, cold, pain or proprioception (position sense). Pain may be experienced without any tissue damage, because pain neurones are triggered at concentrations of noxious agents equivalent to half of the concentration that would produce tissue injury.

Similarities exist between internal and external modification of communications of pain. Hot compresses or massage seem to help with pain by flooding internal processing centres with attention-capturing stimuli, resulting in attention to the alternate stimuli, and therefore distraction from the painful stimuli. This is a similar mechanism to hypnosis and relaxation techniques, which direct attention towards other non-painful areas and neuronal signals. These processes are dependent upon 'gate control' in which non-painful signals can block painful stimuli at the spinal cord (Figure 2.1). Local anaesthetics ease perceived pain by blocking the conduction of the peripheral impulse long before it reaches the

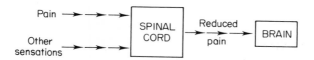

Figure 2.1 Gate control of pain

brain. Analgesics such as opiates act centrally by changing the interpretation of signals from pain neurones.

When a series of painful impulses are brought to the level of conscious awareness, children initiate an investigation by enhanced attending to other sensations from the same area, by touching the area with a hand, and by using other senses, particularly vision (Figure 2.2). All this information is then filtered through their current emotional state, determined mainly by their social and physical context, and their personal past experience, as they attempt to assign significance to the signal. This strategy is quite effective for investigating the skin and other anatomically superficial structures when confirming or excluding the presence of a potentially injurious agent. It is, however, a poor strategy for the investigation of painful or questionable stimuli from internal organs. Thus determining the significance of pain from deep structures is more difficult for the child.

At this juncture, the child usually informs an adult about internal pain. All the information is filtered through the adult's current emotional state, attitudes

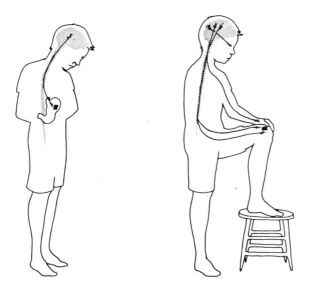

Figure 2.2 Sorting out pain—internal process

and self-concepts, as well as personal past experiences of pain and children in pain, as they attempt to assign significance to the child's communication of pain. The adult moulds the child's response and attitudes towards internal sensations, externally communicated as pain. Anxious or insecure adults are often unable to judge the overall well-being of the child, and when confronted with a child's complaints of deep pain, psychosocial factors pertaining to the adult greatly influence the assessment.

The past experience and fantasies of both individuals are potential causes for the pain, even as the investigations and communications are being made. For example, the possibilities considered by the adult/child pair for chest pain are quite different if the child's father had died of a crushing chest injury received during an automobile accident, than a dyad whose closest male relative had died of a heart attack, and different still from the couple unfamiliar with either chest condition. Experience of serious medical conditions, and states of heightened parental anxiety, greatly increase the likelihood of medical consultation for complaints of pain by a child.

The basic approach of a medical expert to problem-solving does not differ substantially from that of parent or child, i.e. he starts by considering likely causes, then confirms or rejects them. However, the physician's list of possibilities and methods of searching are much more relevant and refined (Barrows, 1980). The medical expert's opinion and actions are determined by training, personal attributes, external factors such as the parent's concern, and the recent array of clinical cases coming under the expert's care. In an effort to supplement the existing information, the worried medical expert will use diagnostic laboratory and X-ray procedures much more often in cases of head, chest or abdominal pain than pain in more superficial structures.

Pursuing these procedures often reinforces the anxieties of the parent and child, and results in increasing external communications of pain. At this juncture the thought and conversation in the family often follows this line, 'If it's not serious like he said, then why is he ordering all these blood tests and X-rays?' (Figure 2.3).

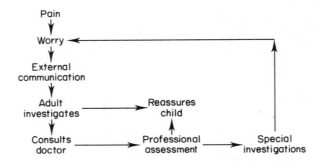

Figure 2.3 Sorting out pain—external process

Whether the pain is benign or serious cannot always be easily or convincingly resolved, and the ensuing anxiety contributes to a vicious cycle, emphasizing the importance of early and clear diagnosis. In some cases unresolved symptoms generate secondary gain (see Chapter 1) and further fuel for the circular process. The secondary gain, together with sensitizing past experiences and high anxiety levels in family members, diminishes the communicative value of pain. In chronic pain syndromes nearly all the signal value of pain is lost; parents and physicians often fail to recognize this devaluation and continue to search for noxious agents (Barr, 1983).

Pain syndromes are discussed in detail in Chapter 3.

2.3 BIOLOGICAL SUBSTRATE

In Chapter 1 we introduced the various components of the psychosomatic approach: developmental, biological, psychological, social and family. In this section we examine the relevance of the biological substrate. In general, the portion of the total illness contributed by the biological component varies among different conditions (see Figure 1.1) so as to form a continuum anchored by traditional medical illnesses where biological factors predominate (e.g., bacterial meningitis in a 2-week-old infant) and psychiatric disorders where biological factors make a minor contribution to the total illness. Midway between these two are conditions with significant contributions from each component. It is in these latter illnesses that the concept of biological substrate is important. Most commonly such disorders involve the cardiovascular, pulmonary and gastrointestinal systems, because of their autonomic nervous system innervation (see Section 2.4).

The potential variation in relative contribution of biological, social and psychological factors is illustrated in Figure 2.4 (for the sake of simplicity in this diagram we have subsumed 'developmental' under 'biological' and 'family' under 'social'). This concept of biopsychosocial mapping is described further by Rosse (1984).

The clinical manifestations and particular tissue involved in the pathological process in a given individual, or family, tend to be constant, and seem to be determined by genetically defined tissue susceptibility and/or genetically ordained patterns of autonomic nervous system activity. Thus a kinship may contain multiple children and adolescents who have inherited highly reactive bronchial tubes and respiratory epithelial cells (the biological substrate), and therefore wheeze when sufficiently stressed by physical, social and/or psychological factors. Biologically determined susceptibility exists in most illnesses: ulcerative colitis (intestinal mucous membranes), rheumatoid arthritis (synovial linings and articular surfaces), hypertension (systemic blood vessel walls), migraine (cranial blood vessels), peptic ulcer (acid-secreting gastric mucosa),

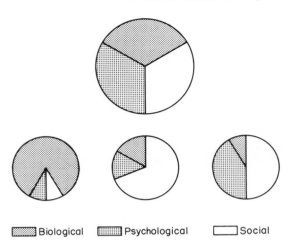

Figure 2.4 Contributions to illness

urticaria (blood vessel permeability), encopresis (anal sphincter function) and so on. Although this concept is useful, the exact mechanisms of the susceptibility may have little to do with actual vulnerability of symptom-producing tissue, and more to do with excessive internal production of agents that over-stimulate, or otherwise adversely affect the tissue in question.

The response of the tissues depends on their physiological characteristics. For example, the gastric mucosa in susceptible individuals increases its secretion of gastric acid, which enters the duodenum with gastric emptying. The mucous membrane in the duodenum (compared to that of the stomach) is ill-equipped to tolerate the acidity. If the excess acidity persists for any length of time, an area of mucous membrane will disintegrate, resulting in a peptic ulcer. In similar fashion, respiratory tract epithelium (which normally secretes fluid to keep the linings from becoming dry) may be stimulated to increase fluid production and bronchial muscle contraction (this muscle action normally varies the diameter of the bronchi between inhalation and exhalation). Both these actions reduce the size of the airway, resulting in wheezing and an asthma attack. In these two examples normal physiological action of a tissue is exaggerated in response to stress, and a pathological condition results.

Typically, multiple and varying factors act in concert to produce a symptomatic episode, but usually the specific symptoms remain the same. Thus a child with a hyperactive bronchus will have an asthma attack in response to a range of different stressors. This narrow range of responses to stress runs through families and across time. Exceptions to this consistency during childhood do exist, such as the shift in tissue type, and site of pathology from skin to bronchi to nasal mucous membranes, seen in atopic (allergic) illness. In this and other disorders where patterns of tissue susceptibility are found, age of the individual seems to be the factor that drives the shift in sites of symptom origin. Thus, in families containing individuals with atopic illness, the typical pattern is: infants manifest eczema (dermal); children show asthmatic symptoms (respiratory— bronchial); and adolescents have allergic rhinitis (respiratory—nasal).

Similarly, age often determines the type of stress-related gastrointestinal disorder. Apley (1982) has shown that pyloric stenosis and colic predominate in infancy; constipation, encopresis and diarrhoea are most common in the toddler years (age 1–3); whilst recurrent abdominal pain and vomiting are in the preponderance during school years. Peptic ulcer, inflammatory bowel disease and anorexia nervosa become more common in adolescence.

Atopic (allergic) disease is a convenient paradigm to explore the permutations of the biological substrate and multifactorial causality. Asthma is a very common problem in primary and preschool-age children. Typically the condition becomes manifest when the load of various stressors (physical or emotional) reaches a critical level. Accordingly, any combination of specific allergens (e.g., cat fur), a non-specific pulmonary irritant (e.g., cigarette smoke), exercise, respiratory infection and stress may combine so that the child eventually becomes symptomatic (Figure 2.5). Reciprocally decreasing the exposure to any of these factors may be sufficient to bring about clearing of symptoms, although the load of the other factors remains. This summation of psychological stress, physical stress and genetically determined tissue vulnerability is typical of many more illnesses than those which have traditionally been labelled 'psychosomatic'.

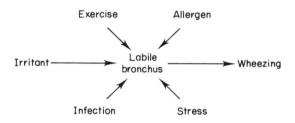

Figure 2.5 Contributions to asthma

2.4 EMOTIONAL AROUSAL AND SYMPATHETIC NERVOUS SYSTEM ACTIVITY

The autonomic nervous system (ANS) controls the organs, glands and smooth muscles responsible for involuntary, self-regulating functions such as circulation and gut motility. One branch, the sympathetic, is mainly responsible for the 'fight or flight' reaction, whilst the parasympathetic branch has in general an opposite, calming and restorative effect (Winefield and Reay, 1980). Usually the two branches are antagonistic and the state of the body reflects the balance between them. This balance is mainly determined by personality attributes and environmental factors.

In situations of fear or anger, the various systems and organs of the body are automatically prepared for action by the ANS. The affect-related changes are obvious to anyone following a frightening experience, and include trembling hands, sweating or a pounding heart. These are brought about by circulating adrenaline, which is released by the action of the sympathetic portion of the autonomic system on the adrenal gland, and by the release of noradrenaline at nerve endings in target organs. The important components of this phenomenon are: pupil dilatation; increased voluntary muscle tone; increased heart rate and stroke volume; increased blood vessel tone; decreased intestinal and urinary bladder tone, with increased rectal and bladder sphincter tone; elevation of circulating white cell counts; glucose release from liver stores; and shunting of blood flow away from abdominal organs toward muscle and brain.

During childhood, culturally dependent restraints are taught and modelled by parents and other important authority figures, which place certain restrictions on behaviour. The majority of these restrictions are quite beneficial for the individual and the group in most situations. However, one exception, the inhibition of immediate release of anger, has important complications for the health of many individuals. Because strongly felt anger (or anxiety) is automatically coupled with physiological preparation for extreme exertion, the inhibiting of the release of such emotions may leave the body in a prolonged state of alertness. Under these circumstances, chronic sympathetic nervous system arousal would bring prolonged excessive smooth (involuntary) and striated (voluntary) muscle activity.

Examples of clinical conditions associated with this state of perpetual readiness are palpitations from stimulation of the cardiac pacing mechanism and muscle, hypertension from increased cardiac and blood vessel wall muscular activity, and tension headaches from prolonged neck muscle contractions. An additional important example is recurrent mild diabetic ketoacidosis in juvenile diabetics. In this situation the children are distressed by the family and have no way of releasing their feelings. This leads to sustained elevations of adrenaline and blood glucose. The latter eventually leads to diabetic ketoacidosis (Minuchin *et al.*, 1978).

2.5 STRESS AND IMMUNITY

2.5.1 The physiology of defence

The immune system is not initially involved in defending the body against invasion. Initial and major protective mechanisms exist in the skin and mucous membranes (e.g., nasal mucosa) at the interface between the body and external world. These surfaces form quite effective physical barriers to invasion under most circumstances. At sites of particular vulnerability, these defensive barriers are augmented by secretions and self-cleaning mechanisms, which tend to keep the immediate environment free of toxic organisms. For example, warm externally communicating tubes, such as sinuses, external and middle ear canals, lungs and urinary tract, are especially vulnerable to invasions by microorganisms. In these sites acidity, cerumen, mucous secretion and/or ciliary sweeping tend to suppress microorganisms and enhance tubular cleansing. Although the immune system may participate in such defence (through the inclusion of immune system synthesized protein with antibody activity, IgA, in secretions), generally it only becomes operational if the perimeter defences have been breached. Numerically this is a small portion of the total work of defending the body from infection.

Once the perimeter has been penetrated, cellular and chemical safeguards come into play. Initially tissue-bound and circulating phagocytic cells will ingest and kill organisms. If penetrating organisms are few, this effort might be completely successful, and in that scenario no infection or sign of disease develops. However, if the penetrating organism is able to reproduce and establish itself inside the body, some ingesting phagocytes will present antigens from the invading organism to precursors of antibody-producing immunological cells. The latter cells will multiply, mature, and begin producing antibodies that attack the invading organism. Concurrently some of the selected precursors cells are set aside against the chance that the same organism might penetrate the body again.

The result of the organism–antibody reactions is direct lysis (death) of the intruder, or facilitation of much more efficient (enhanced) phagocytosis. On the occasion of a second penetration of the same organism, circulating antibodies react with its surface and greatly enhance clearing of the organism. Subsequent to this second exposure, high levels of circulating antibodies are produced (amnestic response) and the body becomes immune to further attacks by that organism.

The interactions and chemical signals of the immunological cascade are quite complex, and at least one group of these chemicals (lymphokines) seem to penetrate the central nervous system and affect modulation of neuroendocrine function and behaviour (Calabrese *et al.*, 1987).

2.5.2 The impact of stress

There is now considerable evidence that the immunological response (but not the perimeter barrier defences) is modified by psychosocial stress (Editorial, 1987). Findings indicate that immunological cells from recently bereaved (and perhaps lonely and distressed) individuals could not be stimulated to multiply to the same extent as those from matched normal controls and that there was a reduction in natural killer cell activity. These findings are largely limited to bereaved individuals with significant depressive symptoms. Numbers of circulating phagocytes and levels of circulating antibodies do not seem to be affected (Baker, 1987).

Epidemiological evidence points to an association between stress and increased susceptibility to death among cancer patients, which may be mediated by the immunological system. Similar evidence connects stress and increased rates of streptococcal infection and infectious mononucleosis (Haggerty, 1982). 'Autoimmune diseases', especially rheumatoid arthritis, are highly correlated in timing of onset and remission with stressful life events (Editorial, 1985). Although the physiological mechanisms of these associations have not been clarified, and many unconfirmed findings exist, the evidence for communication between the central nervous system and the immune system seems to be overwhelming.

2.6 SUMMARY

(1) Most illnesses have multiple contributory factors which interact in a complex and only partially understood manner.
(2) The relative contribution of psychological, social and biological factors varies depending on the disorder, but in all instances each requires due consideration.
(3) Insights into complex psychophysiological mechanisms have been introduced through a discussion of four well-understood pathways: pain, biological substrates, the autonomic nervous system, and stress and the immune system.

CHAPTER 3

Clinical Features—Themes and Variations

Physical growth does not cause pain, but emotional growth can hurt like hell (Apley, 1963)

GUIDE FOR THE READER

This chapter involves an exploration of the amazingly varied world of somatic manifestations of stress and distress. It should not be read in one go, but rather dipped into, or referred to as the occasion demands. Treatment is not discussed in detail as later chapters focus on the different types of therapy, but guidelines are offered to the more useful approaches for each problem.

3.1 INTRODUCTION

In primary care settings 30% of patients have a diagnosable psychiatric disorder and around 20% present with somatic complaints (Lipowski, 1987). The incidence in children is probably much higher. In general paediatric clinics somatization disorders are diagnosed in about half of all cases (Apley, 1982; Smithells, 1982; Wolff, 1986). Even in a non-clinical population one in ten schoolchildren suffer from non-organic recurrent abdominal pain. Whilst organic causes must be excluded the physician should be wary of 'Becoming a pathogenic agent in his well-meaning but never-ending efforts to find a physical cause' (Apley, 1963).

It is only for the sake of convenience that we have categorized the various disorders in this chapter. Such distinctions are inevitably artificial, given the degree of overlap between symptoms. For example, abdominal pain is often accompanied by nausea, vomiting or headache, whilst enuresis may be a frequent companion of failure to thrive. Some problems are considered in more depth in Chapter 4, which focuses on adaptation to illness. In as much as distinctions are possible, we have considered most disorders in terms of their demography, clinical features, differential diagnosis, physical examination and

investigations, management and outcome. The problems discussed are predominantly those whose manifestations are primarily physical, although the
causes are more in the psychosocial and developmental realms.

3.2 RECURRENT ABDOMINAL PAIN

Between 10 and 20% of schoolchildren experience recurrent abdominal pain,
and only one in twenty of these have an organic cause (Apley *et al.*, 1978). Non-
organic recurrent abdominal pain is therefore probably the single most common
presenting symptom in childhood. It is most frequent in the age group 5–12,
and is equally distributed between boys and girls. There is no difference
between socio-economic classes. Frequently it is accompanied by such symptoms as headache, nausea, vomiting, limb or joint pains.

The abdominal pain may occur as often as daily, for hours at a time, or less
frequently, less regularly and for shorter periods. It rarely occurs at night, and if
it does it is more indicative of an organic cause. Sometimes it occurs at very
specific times, such as Sunday evenings and weekday mornings during school
term, or when parents are arguing. In such instances the causes are fairly
obvious. Not infrequently the pattern is non-specific and the causes are less
obvious.

The *differential diagnosis* is wide, including appendicitis, mesenteric adenitis,
urinary tract infections, Crohn's disease or other inflammatory bowel disorders
and a multitude of other rarer causes of abdominal pain. However, a careful
history and the mandatory physical examination will almost always clarify the
true nature of the pain. *Physical examination and laboratory investigations* tend to
be normal or reveal minor non-specific abnormalities. Suggestions that the pain
is due to lactose intolerance (Wald *et al.*, 1982), or other obscure abnormalities,
lack any convincing evidence (Fenton and Milla, 1988).

Many euphemisms have been used to describe this condition, especially when
accompanied by vomiting and/or headache, including 'irritable bowel syndrome', 'abdominal migraine', 'spastic colon', 'periodic syndrome' and 'cyclical
vomiting'. In general such terms do little to explain the problem but seem to
make the physicians feel better! Parents are often more able to accept a named
condition, even if it does not have an organic cause. Generally, however,
'periodic syndrome' is best reserved for those children who have recurrent
episodes of abdominal pain, headache and vomiting and possibly fever, whilst
'cyclical vomiting' should refer to children with recurrent episodes of dramatic
vomiting often leading to dehydration (see section 3.4). These two conditions
are fairly discrete clinical entities, unlike 'abdominal migraine' and 'spastic
colon', which are terms best abandoned as they serve no useful purpose.

Management consists of a thorough assessment to exclude organic causes as
well as to identify positive indications of emotional problems. Careful explana-

tion and patient discussion with the parents is essential for this, as for all other disorders. Attention is paid to alleviating stress factors, and teaching the child techniques for self-relaxation frequently helps (see Chapter 9). Parents should always be counselled (see Chapter 7), whilst individual therapy for the child (see Chapter 9) or family therapy (see Chapter 8) often relieve the problem. There is little place for medication such as tranquillizers, analgesics, antiemetics or antispasmodics, unless vomiting is severe.

Outcome—about one-third of such children continue to have abdominal pain in adult life, whilst another third develop migraine or recurrent headache (Fenton and Milla, 1988). The remainder 'grow out of it'.

3.3 OTHER PAIN SYNDROMES

Apley (1982) has suggested that the various, recurrent non-organic pains of childhood should be grouped together 'because of the similarities and inter-relationships between the pains, between the children who suffer them, and also between their families. They are expressions of a pattern of reaction to emotional stress, which is often part of a family pattern'.

Chest pain, limb pain, joint pain and headache are all common examples of recurrent non-organic pain in childhood, generally of a similar nature to recurrent abdominal pain. Predisposing factors (Chapter 1) may determine the site of the pain, so that, for example, one child who has suffered a knee injury may experience pain in that joint, whilst another, whose father has recurrent headaches, may develop the same symptom, being genetically or environmentally so predisposed.

There is a high incidence of pain disorder in children, with limb pains affecting up to one in five children, and headache one in seven. In a series of 200 new patients with headache, Jerrett (1979) found 66% had no organic cause. Of children with limb pains, only 3% had an organic cause (Apley *et al.*, 1978). Joint pains are likely to be similar in nature and incidence. Distribution of such pains is equal between the sexes and socio-economic groupings.

The euphemism 'growing pains' has frequently been used to describe limb pains for which no organic cause could be found. Of 213 children who had been so labelled, Naish and Apley (1951) could postulate a physical cause in only seven. It was from this finding that Apley eventually concluded that 'emotional growth can hurt like hell'.

The *natural history* of these pains may vary. A child with pain in, say, the ankle, leg, knee or hip is more likely to experience that pain after exercise (often minimal) whilst headache may occur at any time, although rarely at night. Chest pain is more common in children with a parent who has chest pain. Non-organic back pain is uncommon and pain in the spinal region is more often organic. The age range and gender distribution for these non-organic pains is similar to those of recurrent abdominal pain.

Differential diagnosis is determined by the site of the pain. True migraine (see section 3.8.3) needs to be distinguished from simple headache, for the treatment differs. Cerebral tumours and abscesses, hypertension and short-sightedness are other causes of headache needing exclusion. Chest pain may be indicative of respiratory tract infection or oesophageal reflux, as for example in hiatus hernia, but is rarely due to heart disease (the most likely parental fear). Joint pains may be due to some form of arthritis or, as with limb pains, an inflammatory condition or physical injury.

Physical examination and investigation is usually normal, although occasionally non-specific abnormalities may be found. For example, restricted movement or muscle wasting may be found in joint pain, but it should be remembered that reduced activity (because of pain) may ultimately lead to such findings. Electroencephalograms (EEG) are often carried out as part of the investigation for headache, yet Apley has shown that no fewer than 50 of 200 healthy schoolchildren had abnormal EEGs (Apley, 1982). Old injuries on X-ray should not necessarily be deemed to be the main cause of current limb or joint pain, although these may be predisposing factors.

Management is very similar to that for recurrent abdominal pain, with the same principles applying.

Outcome is reasonable, with complete or long periods of remission of symptoms in the majority of children.

3.4 NAUSEA AND VOMITING

Both nausea and vomiting are very common symptoms in childhood, with a wide range of causes. Most of these are not serious, and include 'tummy upsets', virus infections, travel sickness, excitement and anxiety. It is only if the symptoms persist over time, or recur frequently, that concern is justified.

The pattern of such symptoms tends to vary through the age groups. Infants frequently regurgitate their feeds and this is rarely of any significance. Similarly vomiting in toddlers and pre-school children is common and usually not important. In the older age groups these symptoms are less common and if recurring or persisting do require investigation.

An exception to the rule in infancy is the frequent regurgitation of feeds with (1) *rumination* and, unchecked, failure to thrive. Such infants appear to gain comfort, and possibly previously withheld attention, by ruminating. Rarely is there an organic cause, although occasionally there is present a small hiatus hernia which predisposes the infant to regurgitation. The problem rarely lasts beyond infancy but may be replaced by an eating disorder. (2) *Cyclical vomiting* occurs most commonly in the age range 5–12 and affects boys and girls equally.

It is characterized by recurrent episodes of vomiting, which may last only a few hours, or persist for several days, ultimately leading to dehydration. Rarely is a precipitating cause found, and often there is a phasic quality with its recurring on a regular basis, or as infrequently as once a year. It may be accompanied by pain or fever, although headache may ensue from dehydration. Most children seem to grow out of it, but some develop migraine in adolescence or adult life. (3) *Self-induced vomiting* does occur, usually in adolescence, as one of the features of anorexia nervosa (see section 3.6.4). It is rare in younger age groups, although some children seem able to induce vomiting with relative ease. It is done secretively, rarely admitted to, and is symptomatic of serious underlying emotional problems. The problem may become deeply entrenched and difficult to eradicate.

The *differential diagnosis* of nausea and vomiting is wide, and includes infection, particularly of the gastrointestinal tract, other forms of gastrointestinal pathology, raised intracranial pressure and metabolic disorders. Nausea and vomiting are also side effects of many medications.

Physical examination and investigation of non-organic vomiting reveals only changes secondary to the vomiting, such as dehydration, failure to thrive in infants and toddlers, and weight loss in older children. Secondary electrolyte and metabolic changes will often be found.

Management of the psychological aspects is in principle similar to that of previous disorders discussed. In addition behavioural techniques, such as extinction of rumination by ignoring it but paying increased attention to non-ruminating behaviour, are valuable (see Chapter 9). Antiemetics or antispasmodics are sometimes useful in recurrent or cyclical vomiting, whilst self-induced vomiting must be managed in the context of the wider underlying problem (usually anorexia nervosa).

Rehydration may be necessary in the more severe vomiting, and the depression accompanying dehydration needs to be recognized as such, rather than treated with antidepressants.

Outcome—nausea and vomiting of non-organic origin rarely persist into adult life, except in the occasional case of anorexia nervosa.

3.5 BLADDER AND BOWEL DISORDERS

These are common somatic manifestations of distress, and include enuresis, dysuria, urinary frequency, urinary retention, constipation and diarrhoea.

3.5.1 Enuresis

Enuresis is involuntary micturition after 5 years of age, either nocturnal or diurnal (daytime) or both. Approximately 10% of children are enuretic at the age of 5, 5% at age 10, but only 1% at 15. The incidence is higher in those from a lower socio-economic background, and is twice as high in boys as girls. Enuresis may be primary in that the child has never gained control, or secondary in that previously gained control is lost. A number of factors may predispose to enuresis. There is often a family history of bed-wetting and more often than not the child has been exposed to significant levels of stress in the pre-school years. The child may be delayed in other aspects of development. Unduly harsh or lax parental attitudes to toilet training may also contribute. Precipitating factors include stressful events such as examinations, major arguments, change of school or loss of a friend or relative. Daytime wetting with or without nocturnal enuresis is usually indicative of a more serious disturbance than nocturnal enuresis alone.

3.5.2 Urinary frequency, retention and dysuria

Frequency, retention and dysuria (difficulty or pain when passing urine) are occasionally manifestations of distress. Frequency is a common concomitant of anxiety, as anyone who has ever taken an exam will know. Pain on micturition may be associated with a previous and painful urinary tract infection, and is more common in girls than boys. Such symptoms rarely persist for long in the absence of organic disease. If they do, or if there are recurrent urinary tract infections in the absence of an obvious cause, sexual abuse should be considered (see section 3.11.5). Urinary retention is uncommon but when it does occur organic causes must be excluded.

The differential diagnosis of these urinary problems includes urinary tract infection, renal failure, diabetes mellitus, diabetes insipidus, spinal disorders and sexual abuse.

Physical examination and investigation are nearly all normal in the absence of physical disease. Underlying organic pathology will be demonstrated on routine investigation.

Management is determined by the specific symptoms. Nocturnal enuresis may be treated in a number of different ways. Firstly it is helpful to reassure child and parents that this is a common disorder with no serious cause, and that it will clear up of its own accord eventually. Some helpful simple measures include restricting fluid intake to 4 hours before bedtime, omitting any fluids with a diuretic (increasing urinary output) effect, and ensuring bladder emptying at bedtime. Waking the child and taking him to the toilet at the parents' bedtime may also be tried. Regular waking with visits to the toilet during the night is tedious and tiring, but if it ensures a dry bed this builds up the child's confidence. Rewards for dry nights also have a positive effect. Younger children enjoy star charts or their equivalent, whilst older ones might prefer tokens which can be exchanged for a reward when a specific number have been earned.

Enuresis alarms are of value in 80% of cases when practical circumstances allow their use and the child and parents are well motivated to learn the correct techniques (Dische *et al.*, 1983). Failure occurs when there is a lack of motivation or incorrect use of equipment, or when the child sleeps so deeply that he fails to hear the alarm.

The only medication of value in enuresis is the tricyclic range of antidepressants, which work not by their antidepressant effect but either by a specific action on the bladder or by altering sleep rhythm. They are very effective whilst being used, but because of the frequency of relapse when they are withdrawn adjunctive treatments should be used. The usual dose is 25–50 mg (depending on the child's size) of either imipramine or amitriptyline given about 2 hours before bedtime.

Parental counselling will always be necessary, and sometimes individual therapy for the child (Chapter 9) or family therapy (Chapter 8) may be indicated in particularly resistant cases.

Daytime wetting, whilst often indicative of more serious disturbance, is sometimes easier to treat. The most useful approach is that of bladder training, which involves teaching the child to slowly increase the interval between planned bladder emptying. This technique is more likely to succeed if it is done gradually, and is combined with a reward scheme and parental counselling. It should go without saying that contributory factors need to be tackled.

Other urinary symptoms are best managed by directly treating the underlying difficulties.

Outcome—virtually all such urinary problems resolve spontaneously in the course of time, although they may recur intermittently in later years.

3.5.3 Constipation

Constipation involves difficulty or delay in bowel opening, and is most common in the age group 1–3 but may occur at any age, in either sex. In some instances there is an obvious precipitating factor such as an anal fissure (a small but painful tear of the anal mucosa), poor diet or toilet phobia. Alternatively, unduly demanding toilet training, combined with the child's personality and developmental phase, may produce the problem. The harder some parents try to get the child to use the pot, the more some children will resist, with an ensuing 'battle of the bowel'.

Untreated constipation can lead to partial obstruction with consequent leakage of fluid faeces, sometimes mistaken for diarrhoea or deliberate soiling.

Differential diagnosis includes Hirschsprung's disease, in which there is a lack of ganglion cells in the internal sphincter and subsequent failure to evacuate. The constipation is usually present from birth.

Physical examination is essential in constipation to exclude anal fissure and Hirschsprung's disease. An anal fissure is usually visible, whilst in the latter there is very marked abdominal distension. Rectal examination usually indicates the depth of the constipation. *Plain X-ray* of the abdomen will demonstrate the amount of faeces in the colon, and the presence or absence of distended loops will help clarify the existence of Hirschsprung's disease. A rectal biopsy will confirm or refute that diagnosis.

Management of constipation involves the treatment of any underlying organic factors, and of the constipation per se. No psychological treatments can work whilst the rectum (and colon) are loaded with faeces. Dietary manipulation alone is usually insufficient, and laxatives are usually necessary (see Chapter 10). In resistant cases suppositories or even enemas may be required. Prolonged conservative treatment rarely works and only serves to demoralize the child and parents, and to reduce confidence in the physician. Far better to encourage a rapid (if somewhat dramatic) evacuation, so that the psychological treatments may be initiated quickly and with greater chance of success. However successful the physical treatment, it is very likely that the psychological treatments will also be necessary to break the faulty pattern, and that small doses of laxatives will be required to enable the bowel to regain normal functioning.

Parents should be advised to adopt a less demanding approach to toileting. It is useful to institute a programme of regular toileting once or twice a day but with no demands for successful performances! A reward scheme (see Chapter 9) may be helpful. Where a toilet phobia exists a graded desensitization approach (Chapter 9) will be necessary. A structured programme of gradual use of the toilet is drawn up, often starting with simply rewarding the child for entering the room, then for sitting on the toilet without producing anything, and only later expecting normal use of the toilet.

Outcome—the vast majority of constipated children respond well to the appropriate treatment, but all too often treatment is applied in a partial way, ensuring failure. Where correct treatment is ineffective a short period of hospitalization is often sufficient to overcome the problem.

3.5.4 Encopresis

Encopresis is the passage of formed faeces in inappropriate places, such as clothing or the bed. It may broadly be considered as being of three types: (1) primary, (2) secondary, and (3) constipation with overflow. Primary encopresis refers to those situations where satisfactory bowel control has never been achieved, whilst in secondary encopresis there has been a regression from normal control. In both cases the stool is of firm or soft consistency, but clearly distinguishable from constipation with overflow (see section 3.5.3)—the result of massive constipation, in which *fluid* faeces leak past the obstruction.

Encopresis tends to affect children in the age group 3–10, and is rare in adolescence. Boys outnumber girls in the ratio of three or four to one, and children from lower socio-economic background are more likely to be affected.

Primary encopresis is most commonly seen in the pre-school age group, and is usually associated with chaotic and disorganized families in whom toilet training is either lax or absent. *Secondary encopresis* usually occurs a few years after bowel control has been achieved and is invariably a sign that the child is in considerable distress. Commonly such children have been exposed to severe or persisting stress. Many secondary encopretic children have fastidious or obsessional mothers, as if perchance they have found a vulnerable spot. (It is intriguing to note the relationship between parental occupation and/or personality and the child's symptom—for example, we have seen many policemen's children who steal, schoolteachers' children who under-achieve or disrupt the classroom, overweight parents whose children have eating disorders, and over-anxious parents whose children refuse to attend school.)

Occasionally children with secondary encopresis smear their faeces on walls or furniture or deposit them around the home, both activities appearing to be a fairly aggressive act towards the parents! Many encopretic children are ashamed of their problem and try to conceal or deny it, but some seem relatively unperturbed.

The differential diagnosis is the same as that for constipation but also includes all the possible causes of diarrhoea, such as infection, malabsorption and inflammatory bowel disease. Careful history and physical examination are almost invariably sufficient to confirm the diagnosis.

Management is similar to that of constipation. A combined approach paying attention to both physical and psychological factors is usually necessary. If simple behavioural techniques fail, family therapy (Chapter 8) as an adjunct will often serve to clarify and resolve underlying contributory factors.

Outcome for encopresis is usually good.

3.5.5 Diarrhoea

Only rarely does diarrhoea occur in the absence of clear-cut physical disorder. It is usually due to infection, malabsorption, dietary abnormalities or inflammatory bowel disease. Occasionally diarrhoea, as with frequency of urine, occurs as a response to acute anxiety (thus the origin of the crude expression 'shit scared'). A few toddlers suffer diarrhoea for which no cause can be found, and to help calm the physician's concern about this it is labelled '*toddler diarrhoea*'. Generally such children thrive despite the problem, and it usually resolves with time. Similarly some children between the ages of 3 and 8 have frequent bowel movements, often several times a day, for which no organic cause is found. Again these children thrive. The condition is named '*chronic non-specific diarrhoea*' and tends to resolve spontaneously with time. As micro-diagnostic techniques advance it may well be discovered that all these problems are gut-motility disorders due to enzyme or neurological abnormalities. The management of diarrhoea is essentially physical, but underlying psychological problems should be appropriately tackled. Loperamide (see Chapter 10) is the most useful medication.

3.6 DISORDERS OF EATING AND GROWTH

The range of disorders associated with eating and growth may be classified as follows:

(1) feeding problems in young children
(2) failure to thrive
(3) pica
(4) anorexia nervosa
(5) overeating and obesity
(6) polydipsia

3.6.1 Feeding problems in young children

Feeding problems often start very early in life and set the pattern for later difficulties. Some babies are easy to feed, whilst at the other end of the spectrum are those who seem to refuse everything. Most mothers have no problems in feeding their infants but some have a struggle. Such problems may be precipitated or perpetuated by developmental or physical disorders in the baby, or maternal ill health, anxiety or depression.

Toddlers and young children can be very fussy about their food, and parents similarly can be just as fussy about what and how their child should eat. Difficult behaviour around food can try the patience of any parent, but equally, rigid or anxious parents can precipitate feeding problems in children lacking an easy-going temperament. Behaviour that supports inadequate feeding can be identified in about 80% of families who have infants with non-organic failure to thrive (Fosson and Wilson, 1987). These include maternal distress and family chaos.

Food fads and fussiness are commonplace in young children and rarely lead to harm. If parents over-react, however, they may initiate a vicious cycle of anxiety and food refusal. An early example of this is infantile (or 3 months) colic. The baby has episodes of severe pain, usually after an evening feed, lasting up to several hours. The screaming is accompanied by drawing up of the legs. The cause is unknown and there is no evidence that it is induced by maternal anxiety. However, it is possible that the resulting tension and distress may communicate itself to the baby, who then has difficulty with subsequent feeds.

The incidence of feeding problems in young children is unknown because of problems of definition, but they are undoubtedly common, affect both sexes, and are no respecters of social class.

Physical causes for feeding difficulties must be excluded by careful history taking, physical examination and, if necessary, special investigations. Any physical disorder can produce feeding difficulties.

Management requires patient investigation of potential psychosocial factors such as parental anxiety or depression, lack of support for the mother, family conflict and adverse social circumstances. *Treatment* is directed at the contributory psychosocial factors. It is helpful to observe feeds or mealtimes whenever possible so that dysfunctional interactions may be identified and changed (Fosson and Wilson, 1987). Support and, if necessary, counselling or psychiatric treatment should be provided for overwhelmed or disturbed parents. Attempts should be made to help alleviate adverse social conditions and family therapy offered where obvious pathology exists. Behavioural techniques such as reward schemes for eating specified amounts can be helpful for young children. For particularly intractable cases the use of day facilities or hospitalization may be necessary.

Outcome—feeding disorders can be notoriously difficult to overcome, and considerable help over long periods is often required. In general, however, most children overcome their problems, although sometimes remaining rather fussy, poor eaters, and with a tendency to be underweight. A few develop such problems as failure to thrive or anorexia nervosa (see section 3.6.4).

3.6.2 Failure to thrive

Failure to thrive involves a failure to gain weight or height, either at an early age or after a period of normal growth. It can occur in any age group, sex distribution is equal and there is no proven class distinction. Feeding problems often lead to failure to thrive, although sometimes the child appears to be taking normal quantities of food, but vomiting or diarrhoea occur. In some instances food intake is described as satisfactory, and there are no other symptoms to account for the failure to thrive. When some of these children are observed in hospital, their food intake is seen to be inadequate, but a small number are indeed eating normal amounts and yet fail to grow.

The terms 'emotionally determined failure to thrive' and 'psychosocial dwarfism' have been used to describe those children who fail to thrive for no obvious biological reason other than limited dietary intake, and those for whom no cause whatsoever can be found. Clearly, before reaching such a diagnosis, care must be taken to ensure that no organic disorder exists. It may be that distress creates a poor appetite and therefore reduced intake, or that processes concerned with digestion or absorption are impaired. However, intermediaries in the complex process of growth may be deficient (e.g., partial growth hormone deficiency or somatomedin deficiency). There is much yet to be understood in the pathogenesis of failure to thrive, but Skuse (1985) considers that the most likely cause of non-organic failure to thrive is low calorie intake due to parent–child relationship problems. A common cause is emotional abuse, neglect or deprivation (see section 3.11.2).

Management—it is usually best to admit such children to hospital so that careful observation of calorie intake and investigations for organic pathology may be carried out. Nursing staff observations of behaviour, particularly in relation to parents, are valuable in clarifying relationship patterns (Dungar *et al.*, 1986). A multidisciplinary approach to treatment will be necessary (see Chapter 6), but many of the techniques discussed in the previous section will apply. Where emotional abuse has occurred, consideration should be given to alternative forms of care if the existing environment cannot be improved.

3.6.3 Pica

Pica is the ingestion of non-edible substances, such as dirt, sand, buttons, tablets, bleaches, etc., and is associated with severe emotional deprivation or disturbance, and with mental retardation. It is usually accompanied by other behavioural problems.

Management of pica involves treatment of the causative factors, whilst behaviour modification techniques (Chapter 9) may help with children who are mentally handicapped.

3.6.4 Anorexia nervosa

Occurring in childhood and early adolescence, anorexia nervosa consists of a determined food avoidance, and a failure to gain weight at the time of the expected growth spurt, or an actual loss of weight. Two or more of the following features will also be present: a preoccupation with body weight, preoccupation with calories, fear of fatness, distorted body image, purging, self-induced vomiting and excessive exercising. Menstrual periods will either not have started or will have ceased.

In this younger age group the sex ratio is five to one in favour of girls (compared to ten to one in late adolescence and young adults). The incidence is around one in 100 of girls between the ages of 16 and 18. Although the incidence for younger children is not known, there is a suggestion that it is increasing (Fosson *et al.*, 1987). It is now also occurring in lower socio-economic groupings as well as the middle classes, and in children of immigrants from developing countries. Anorectic boys seem to be more concerned with fitness and health than with weight and fat.

There is a wide variation of features both in clinical presentation and in the course of the illness, often leading to a missed diagnosis. Whilst Crohn's disease can be excluded by careful investigation, the clinical picture can be confused with that of depression, cyclical vomiting or school phobia (Fosson *et al.*, 1987). Depression occurs in about 50% of cases, and academic conscientiousness and obsessionality are also often present. Careful history taking and clinical observation will reveal the correct diagnosis.

One of the most striking features is the determined attempt the child makes to control not only her weight but all those around her. If the friendly, appealing approach does not work, then such children resort to determined manipulation or angry and defiant outbursts. The ability to 'split' parents or ward staff is startling.

The aetiology is unknown but is likely to be due to a combination of factors, including (1) concerns with impending sexuality, (2) preoccupations with issues of control, (3) family conflict, and (4) socio-cultural pressures to be thin. No underlying biological substrate has been identified but it has been suggested that the patients have a disturbed perception of somatic sensations such as hunger, and of body size and shape. The possibility of zinc deficiency or hypothalamic dysfunction as causes have been proposed, but it is more likely that in the rare instances where these occur they are secondary to self-starvation rather than the cause of it.

Physical examination reveals dehydration and emaciation in many such children, accompanied by low blood pressure, slow pulse, poor peripheral circulation, cold extremities and the characteristic lanugo hair. There are no special investigations that will specifically identify anorexia nervosa, but there may be a deficiency of protein, copper or zinc.

Management—in all but the mildest cases a multidisciplinary approach (Chapter 6) is essential and hospitalization is usually indicated. It may be easier to assist the children on a psychiatric unit than on a paediatric ward, but if the physicians, nurses and mental health professionals can work together constructively and harmoniously the setting is less important. All staff need to be aware of the child's ability to split and manipulate staff, and to plan the management of all potential problems before they arise (Lask and Bryant-Waugh, 1986).

Working with the family is essential, for invariably there are problems at home which, if unresolved, will impede recovery or hasten relapse. The parents need to work consistently together, communicate openly, and resolve their conflicts without involving the children. Individual psychotherapy may help when the psychopathology is so deeply entrenched that it is not accessible to other forms of therapy. Appetite stimulants are useless, not least because there is often no loss of appetite. Tranquillizers seem not to help, but antidepressants are indicated when depression coexists.

Gradual refeeding should start on admission to hospital and, if life is in danger, nasogastric or intravenous feeding should commence without delay. Rewards for weight gain are often helpful but should only be given for consistent rather than current weight gain, as weight change is so open to manipulation. The rewards should not be linked to parental visits or trips home, as often these children are ambivalent about such events.

Social skills and communication training help the child to find new and healthier ways of expressing distress and coping with concerns about control. Group therapy also assists in the necessary processes of gaining self-awareness and learning new modes of communication.

Outcome—long-term follow-up indicates only a moderate outcome (Bryant-Waugh *et al.*, 1988), with about 60% doing well, and the rest remaining moderately to severely impaired. Mortality in this age group is about 5%. Poor prognostic features include low age of onset, depression and high levels of family dysfunction. Good prognostic features include parental acceptance of the need to work consistently together and to work closely with the medical team, and the ability of the child to move from the stage of food refusal (stage 1) to a second stage of openly and directly expressing anger and the other negative feelings (stage 2) instead of holding them in. More satisfactory eating patterns (stage 3) cannot be gained and maintained until stage 2 has been consolidated.

3.6.5 Overeating and obesity

These problems occur in approximately 10% of children of both sexes and from all social classes. The pattern is often initiated early in life when food is used as a comforter, with the infant's cries having sometimes been misinterpreted as hunger. Commonly there is a family pattern of overeating and obesity. There is often an over-close and rigid relationship between the mother and the obese child, with the eating problem seeming to cement the bond.

Overeating may be perceived as an addiction, in the same manner as alcoholism or drug abuse. The child is addicted to eating, and the family is addicted to its pattern of functioning. Despite the protestations that the child eats very little and the insistence that there must be a 'hormonal' disorder, there is only very rarely an underlying biological explanation. It is true, however, that metabolisms vary, and some children use up fat more slowly than others. However, when the children are admitted to hospital and put on a reducing diet, they lose weight rapidly, except on weekend leave! Obesity is a very difficult condition to overcome and reducing diets on an out-patient basis often fail. A combination of dietary restriction, behaviour modification with frequent rewards for weight loss, and family therapy, would appear to be the best way of tackling this difficult problem. Appetite suppressants are of no value and have dangerous side effects. Hospitalization is indicated when health is at risk.

3.6.6 Polydipsia

Compulsive drinking is rare in children and is usually a symptom of organic disease such as diabetes mellitus, diabetes insipidus or renal failure. Hospitalization for investigation may be necessary to exclude these serious disorders. In their absence polydipsia should be perceived as a behaviour problem similar to overeating, in which the child seems to get comfort in an unhealthy way. Treatment is of any underlying problems as well as the symptom itself. The parents should set reasonable limits on water intake, then slowly return responsibility to the child.

3.7 MOVEMENT DISORDERS

These may be broadly divided into (1) hyperkinesis (2) tics and Tourette's syndrome. Some disorders of movement are considered in section 3.8 as manifestations of more specific problems such as epilepsy or 'hysteria'.

3.7.1 Hyperkinesis

This is characterized by an early onset of grossly over-active behaviour, marked inattention, distractibility and impulsiveness, in most situations, most of the time. In the USA it is more commonly described as attention deficit disorder (ADD), but this term is not used in Britain because it implies a knowledge of psychological processes that is not yet available, and it suggests the inclusion of anxious, preoccupied or apathetic children whose problems are quite different. For similar reasons the term minimal brain dysfunction (MBD) is best avoided. There is no certainty that hyperkinetic children do have minimal brain dysfunction, nor are all children who clearly have evidence of minimal brain dysfunction hyperkinetic.

The incidence of hyperkinesis in Britain is about 0.1% but ADD is diagnosed in the USA in between 5 and 10% of all children (Taylor, 1986). These discrepancies are probably due to difference in definition. Boys are affected three to four times more often than girls. Hyperkinesis is more frequent in families of low socio-economic status (Schacher *et al.*, 1981). Common accompaniments of the main features are aggression, antisocial behaviour, clumsiness, disinhibition and learning difficulties.

The *aetiology* is poorly understood, but usually genetic inheritance, adverse temperament and psychological environment interact to give rise to an immaturity of social and cognitive development (Taylor, 1986). Acquired brain dysfunction due to prenatal and perinatal injuries, and environmental toxins contribute to the hyperactivity of a few individuals. The specificity of the relationship between high lead levels and hyperactive behaviour is not established and is still the subject of vigorous controversy (Smith *et al.*, 1983). The same point applies to the role of additives in diet, and the claims that Feingold (1975) and Egger *et al.* (1985) have made for the value of exclusion diets are far from being substantiated (Taylor, 1986). Abnormalities of the reticular activating system or neurotransmitter mechanisms may also be relevant. At present the best that can be said is that the hyperkinetic syndrome may well embrace several different kinds of neurophysiological abnormality.

Additional contributing factors may include high levels of family discord and aggression, low levels of parental attention, lack of parental control and over-stimulating environments.

The *differential diagnosis* includes more severe forms of brain damage, autism and phenylketonuria, all of which may manifest hyperkinetic behaviour. It is also important to distinguish hyperkinesis, which does require treatment, from 'normal' over-activity which does not. Some children, particularly boys, are blessed with extraordinary amounts of energy and quickly exhaust their parents. There is, however, nothing pathological about such behaviour, providing it is not associated with distractibility, limited attention, disinhibition, learning difficulties or antisocial behaviour.

Physical examination—there are no findings specific to this disorder, and neurological soft signs such as poor coordination or minor congenital anomalies occur no more often than in children with conduct disturbance. Similarly there are no specific findings on special investigation. A substantial proportion have abnormal but non-specific EEG recordings (Taylor, 1986), as do as many as 25% of all children (Apley, 1963).

Management—a number of different approaches are necessary in this trouble-some disorder. The most useful form of medication is methylphenidate (ritalin) in gradually increasing doses. Because of side effects it is wise to institute 'drug holidays', omitting medication at weekends. It may be necessary to maintain such treatment for up to two years, but caution should be taken that growth is not being impaired (one of the possible side effects). Phenothiazines such as chlorpromazine or haloperidol have a calming effect but have unpleasant and sometimes dangerous side effects and are best avoided, unless used for very brief periods.

Parental counselling is always necessary, for the parents are usually in despair. They need to know that hyperkinesis is a biologically determined disorder, and that they have not caused the problem. Equally, however, their style of management can have a crucial effect. The more intolerant and punitive they become the less chance there is of helping their child to cope with the handicap. They should be advised on how to structure the child's environment so that he is not expected to persevere with a task for longer than he is able, and nor should the surroundings be too stimulating. A disorganized, noisy and active environment can only aggravate the problem, whereas calm, controlled and neutral surrounds can have a calming effect. These same points apply to school. Hyperkinetic children should be placed in small classes where there is considerable individual attention.

Behaviour modification techniques (Chapter 9) can be applied both at home and at school. Specified behaviour targets are selected and rewards given for their achievement, whilst as little attention as possible is paid to undesirable behaviour. A combination of behaviour modification with medication and counselling is probably the most useful approach to treatment.

Dietary manipulation has its supporters but evidence is unconvincing. However, when there is a history of allergy in the child or family, an additive-free diet may have some benefit. The more dramatic forms of dietary restriction (Egger *et al.*, 1985) are of dubious value, tedious to apply, and have dangers. They should only be used under the guidance of an experienced dietician (Taylor, 1986).

Outcome—although the hyperactivity may modify in adolescence, some such children become restless and exhaust adults. Antisocial behaviour is often a sequel, and a variety of other social and personality difficulties may occur.

3.7.2 Tics and Tourette's syndrome

Tics are sudden, involuntary and purposeless muscle movements. They can be localized to one muscle group or generalized to several. They may be transient or persistent. Muscle groups most commonly affected are in the face, neck, trunk and limbs. Occasional vocalizations may also occur in the form of grunting or 'barking', shouting or throat clearing. Tourette's syndrome is a rare but handicapping condition consisting of complex tics, vocalizations and coprolalia (swearing). Obsessional behaviour is a common accompaniment.

Tics affect up to 10% of children, with a sex ratio of two or three to one in favour of boys. There is no social class distinction. Mean age of onset is usually around 7 years. Tourette's syndrome, which has an incidence of less than one in a thousand, is usually diagnosed between ages 10 and 15 (Shapiro and Shapiro, 1981). The cause is unknown but is likely to be a combination of factors, including genetic influence, neurological abnormalities and external stress. There is frequently a family history of tics, and non-specific EEG abnormalities are common. Stress, such as family tensions or school pressures, is often present. Local irritants such as respiratory tract infection or short-sightedness often seem to precipitate episodes.

Differential diagnosis—tics need to be distinguished from chorea, tremor and dystonia (Shapiro and Shapiro, 1981) and certain forms of epilepsy. This is readily done in that tics are rapid and transient, unaccompanied by other underlying neurological disorder and disappear during sleep.

Physical examination reveals no other abnormality than the tics, and investigations reveal nothing unusual, other than an abnormal EEG in a minority of cases.

Management—as tics are usually a manifestation of anxiety, identification and alleviation of underlying stresses pays dividends. Relaxation techniques or mass practice (Chapter 9) are often helpful. It is important to advise the parents of the true nature of the problem and caution them against either paying excess attention or adopting a punitive approach. Indeed, the less attention that is paid, the greater the likelihood of spontaneous resolution. However, teasing at school may aggravate the problem, and the child will need advice on how to deal with this.

Medication (Chapter 10) is helpful in resistant cases, and the most suitable agents are pimoside and clonidine. Haloperidol has potentially powerful side effects and is best avoided. Children with Tourette's syndrome are usually so handicapped by the disorder that hospitalization is indicated for full assessment and trials of therapy.

Outcome is good for mild tics, although occasional and brief relapses may occur. Children with complex or multiple tics and with Tourette's syndrome may do much less well, and some children with the latter disorder remain severely impaired.

3.8 NERVOUS SYSTEM DISORDERS

These are classified as follows: (1) psychogenic disorders of movement and sensation ('hysterical disorders'); (2) faints, seizures and pseudoseizures; (3) migraine.

3.8.1 Psychogenic disorders of movement and sensation

This group of disorders is more commonly described as 'hysteria', but the frequent misuse of this term and its pejorative nature make it undesirable. The International Classification of Diseases, 10th revision (ICD 10), developed through the World Health Organization, has dropped the term 'hysteria' and refers instead to 'dissociative disorders of movement and sensation', in which there is a loss of, or alteration in, functioning of movements or of sensations. The movements or sensations are changed or lost, so that the patient presents as having a physical disorder, although no disorder can be found to explain the symptoms. The symptoms can often be seen to represent the patient's concept of physical disorder, which may be at variance with physiological or anatomical principles. For example, some patients lose sensation in their hands and/or feet (glove and stocking anaesthesia) but the nerve supply to these areas would not allow for such a circumscribed anaesthesia.

The terms 'dissociative' and 'conversion' developed from the presumption that the psychological mechanisms operating in these disorders were the dissociation of one part of the individual from the rest, or the conversion of emotional conflict into physical symptoms. Neither is totally satisfactory, and certainly 'conversion' could in these terms apply to any form of somatization. The word 'functional' is also sometimes used, but usually meaning non-organic. Again, this is too vague. The ideal term has yet to be found.

The rest of this section refers to those disorders in which there is a loss or alteration in functioning of movements or sensations (disorders involving additional symptoms such as pain are dealt with in section 3.3). These conditions are relatively unusual in childhood and rare below 8 or 9 years old. The incidence rises sharply in adolescence, and in this age group girls are affected far more commonly than boys. There is no social class distinction.

Disorders of movement may present as a limp or complete inability to walk, or loss of use of part, or all, of an arm. The dysfunction may be partial or complete, and various or variable degrees of incoordination may be evident, resulting in bizarre gaits or inability to stand unaided. Faints and seizures may also occur (see section 3.8.2). Aphonia (loss of voice) is uncommon.

Disorders of sensation usually present as loss of feeling in circumscribed parts of the body, or paraesthesiae (tingling, pins and needles), which may be due to hyperventilation (see section 3.9.2), or partial or complete loss of vision (a rare phenomenon—0.3% of all children seen in a large ophthalmology clinic). Disorders of taste, smell and hearing are even rarer. Amnesia (loss of memory) as a psychogenic disorder is very unusual in childhood.

Differential diagnosis includes a very wide range of central nervous system disorders which can be extremely difficult to exclude. The diagnosis of psychogenic disorder of movement or sensation should *never* be made without a full physical examination and, if in doubt, thorough investigation. The dilemma is that whilst such disorders may warrant complex and potentially harmful investigations, the physician can inadvertently aggravate the problem if a halt is not finally called. Concern that organic disease could be missed is justified, as various investigators have found that a significant minority of conditions diagnosed as 'hysterical' ultimately turn out to have organic disease (Rivinus *et al.*, 1975).

Differentiating organic from psychogenic disorder may be assisted by knowing that disguised organic disease is often accompanied by deteriorating school performance, visual loss, postural abnormalities or variability of symptoms (Rivinus *et al.*, 1975). In contrast, psychogenic disorders usually have a more rapid onset of symptoms, a more frequent family history of 'hysterical' symptoms, and there is often a person in the child's family or peer group with similar symptoms. There is nearly always a discrepancy between the symptoms and the findings at clinical examination (Goodyer and Taylor, 1985; Dubowitz and Hersov, 1976). It is also important to look positively for features of non-organic illness, such as a history of important events in the child's life, major family problems (often denied or concealed) or other forms of serious stress (Thomson and Sills, 1988).

Management—having made a confident diagnosis and helped the parents accept it (Chapter 6), further organic investigation is halted. Where there is dysfunction of movement, physiotherapy offers both physical and psychological benefit. Muscle wasting is avoided, mobilization is encouraged, and the child is given a 'face-saver'. Wherever possible, underlying contributory factors should be explored and resolved by family therapy. It is unwise to put too much pressure on the child to improve. Rather she should be allowed to recover at her own pace. Admission to hospital (either on a paediatric or child psychiatric unit) is often necessary.

Outcome—most children make a full symptomatic recovery (Gratton-Smith *et al.*, 1988) but other problems may emerge, necessitating further treatment. Early diagnosis and close liaison between paediatricians, physiotherapists and child psychiatrists are necessary if prolonged handicap is to be avoided (Leslie, 1988).

3.8.2 Seizures, pseudoseizures and altered consciousness

The presence of seizures or episodes of altered consciousness has a most detrimental effect on the child and family. The nature of the symptoms is terrifying, as personal accounts testify (Chadwick and Usiskin, 1987). There is a higher rate of psychiatric disorder in children with epilepsy and their families than for other diseases, and the problems with which the family have to contend are enormous (Lask, 1988a). These issues are discussed further in Chapter 4. It is not surprising that there is a complex interaction between psychological, social and biological factors whenever there is disorder involving alteration or loss of consciousness.

Differentiating between the different types of seizure disorder is in itself a complex task, for there are many different types, including grand mal, petit mal, drop attacks, temporal lobe epilepsy, temporal lobe syndrome, psychomotor seizures, pseudocoma, stupor, fugues and faints. There are subtle distinctions between all these disorders and anyone dealing with such problems must have a full understanding of them. An excellent description is provided by Lishman (1987). In summary:

Grand mal seizures involve major, generalized convulsions after a brief warning (aura), followed by a loss of consciousness, with limb twitching, jaw clenching and sometimes urinary incontinence.
Petit mal seizures are brief 'absences', lasting a few seconds, with no warning.
Drop attacks involve sudden, profound and generalized relaxation of muscles, so that the patient falls to the ground. They only last for a few seconds.
Temporal lobe epilepsy has a wide variety of manifestations, including abnormal motor behaviour and sensory experiences, but arising from temporal lobe pathology.
Temporal lobe syndrome is a poorly defined concept. The term is not widely used, but tends to refer to persisting changes in behaviour and sensation, including loss of appetite, apathy, disturbances in temperature regulation and abnormal sensory experiences.

Episodic dyscontrol is characterized by uncontrolled outbursts of rage and aggression, usually with minimal or no provocation, associated with occasional aura and other sensory abnormalities, followed by profound remorse.

Pseudoseizures mimic other types of seizure but an organic basis is usually absent, and the EEG tends to be normal.

Pseudocoma is manifested by an apparent loss of consciousness but, in contrast to true coma, the eyes resist passive opening, and movements in response to stimulation are purposeful (e.g., withdrawal of limb in response to painful stimulus).

Stupor is a state of akinesis (lack of movement) and mutism, but with relative preservation of conscious awareness.

Fugues involve complex, extended and integrated abnormal behaviours, without severe impairment of consciousness, such as tending to wander away. The patient appears vague, perplexed and incoherent and the state may last for several days.

Faints are sudden, transient losses of consciousness without seizure phenomena.

Tics and other movement disorders are easily differentiated by careful history-taking and observation.

Whilst most of these disorders very evidently have an organic basis, it is not always possible to decide whether organic or psychogenic factors are mainly to blame and, as with all problems, careful consideration must be given to biological, social and psychological elements. An either/or approach is likely to lead either to the wrong diagnosis or an inadequately controlled condition. The precise diagnosis is not always clear but the same principles apply.

Specific management depends upon the condition but, besides any physical treatment, full attention should be paid to understanding the contribution of psychosocial factors, and alleviating these as much as possible. Adjustment to seizure disorders is discussed in Chapter 4, whilst specific approaches are described in succeeding chapters.

3.8.3 Migraine

This is characterized by recurrent attacks of headache, widely variable in intensity, frequency and duration, commonly unilateral, often associated with nausea or vomiting, visual or other sensory aura, and photophobia (Lishman, 1987). A family history is common. In childhood, migraine rarely starts before age 9 or 10, and its exact incidence is unknown because of misuse of diagnosis.

Migraine attacks are precipitated by various factors, including stress, excitement, exercise and specific foods such as chocolate or cheese. It is often difficult to differentiate between migraine and other types of headache (see section 3.3) but, as with so many disorders, it is unhelpful to adopt an 'either organic or psychological' approach. Serious organic disease such as hypertension and neurological disorders must be excluded by physical examination and, if necessary, special investigations such as EEG, skull X-ray and brain scan. In the majority of cases these will all be negative.

Management involves a dual approach. Physical relief of symptoms can be achieved using either analgesics or more specific antimigraine medication such as ergotamine, whilst elimination of obvious food triggers from the diet may help. There is little support as yet for the view of Egger *et al.* (1983) that an oligoantigenic diet is of value, especially as such an approach is hazardous and rather impractical.

More useful is exploration and alleviation of underlying contributory factors, combined with teaching self-relaxation techniques (Chapter 9).

3.9 RESPIRATORY SYSTEM DISORDERS

We consider (1) cough, (2) hyperventilation, (3) breath-holding, and (4) wheezing.

3.9.1 Cough

The vast majority of coughs have a clearly recognized underlying organic cause, such as asthma, respiratory tract infection or foreign body. Occasionally, however, no cause can be found, as in the case example in Chapter 1, and although the cough may initially have been a symptom of infection there is now no current evidence of disease. Such 'psychogenic' coughs can range from mild to debilitating, and can last from as little as a day to as long as several months. There are no detailed studies available, but clinical experience indicates an equal sex and social class distribution, and an age range from about 8 to 15.

Almost always there are underlying psychosocial stresses, and alleviation of these factors is essential. In most respects it is helpful to consider psychogenic coughs as similar to tics. However, they can be very exhausting, and sedation and even hospitalization may sometimes be necessary.

3.9.2 Hyperventilation

Overbreathing is not a particularly common problem in childhood and the literature is sparse. Sometimes the symptom is very evident, whereas in other cases it goes unrecognized. How obvious the symptom is will depend on the rapidity and depth of breathing. It may be a sign of serious ill health, such as diabetic coma or pre-coma, or aspirin overdose, and it is occasionally a side-effect of sulthiame (an anticonvulsant). In the absence of an organic cause it is likely to be an idiosyncratic and short-lived symptom of anxiety. Persisting hyperventilation eventually causes tetany, due to a lowering of arterial levels of carbon dioxide, with resultant tingling sensations and spasm of the joints of the hand, or rarely feet (carpopedal spasm), stridor, and ultimately convulsions. Clearly hyperventilation leading to tetany will be within the differential diagnosis for any of these problems.

Management involves attempting to understand and alleviate the underlying causes. In handling the immediate problem it is better to avoid paying attention to the symptom, but rather to distract the child and respond to less disturbed behaviour.

3.9.3 Breath-holding

This commonly occurs in the toddler and pre-school age group as an expression of rage or frustration, and is often associated with temper tantrums. Very occasionally it is a response to anxiety or fear. Most episodes are short-lived and harmless. A minority of children go blue before taking a breath, and, very rarely indeed, loss of consciousness or a convulsion occurs. Management involves once again understanding and treating underlying causes. The actual episodes are best ignored, to avoid reinforcing the behaviour, but if the child does turn blue a gentle slap or some other aversive stimulus should remedy the problem.

3.9.4 Wheezing

This rarely occurs in the absence of asthma, a foreign body or a respiratory tract infection. It may be a response to distress in a child with respiratory disease, and the psychological adjustment to such disorders is discussed in the next chapter. There is a complex relationship between psychosocial and biological aspects of asthma which requires careful investigation and management (Lask, 1982a).

3.10 SKIN DISORDERS

The problems considered in this section are (1) eczema, (2) alopecia, (3) trichotillomania, and (4) dermatitis artefacta.

3.10.1 Eczema

This often distressing condition is almost always an allergic response in which there is dryness and scaling of the skin, with intense itching. The subsequent scratching frequently worsens the problem and may lead to infection. Principles relevant to the understanding and management of psychosocial aspects are similar to those which apply to any other chronic or intermittent disorder, such as asthma, and are discussed in detail in Chapter 4. The constant itching, scratching and unsightliness are causes of considerable distress for the child and the family, and this often exacerbates a vicious cycle.

3.10.2 Alopecia

Loss of hair is uncommon in childhood. Cytotoxic drugs for the treatment of malignant disease invariably lead to a loss of hair, but often the cause is unknown. In alopecia areata, which is characterized by localized patches of complete hair loss, it is probable that stress is one of several causative factors, including autoimmunity and heredity. Rarely there is a total loss of body hair (alopecia totalis), which is probably an extreme version of alopecia areata. Some skin diseases which may cause partial alopecia need to be excluded, and hair-pulling is discussed in the next section.

Whether or not hair loss is temporary or permanent, partial or total, the effect on children should not be underestimated. They have to cope with an altered self-image and appearance, anxiety about whether their hair will return and, worst of all, teasing. Wigs and fashionable head-gear may be used to advantage, and every effort should be made to identify and remedy contributory stresses.

Outcome is to some extent dependent on cause. Hair growth returns on cessation of cytotoxic drugs or improvement in any underlying skin disease, such as eczema. In those instances where the cause is unknown, hair sometimes regrows and other times not. With skilled help many children learn to cope with their unusual appearance. As in other disorders it can be helpful to ask famous or popular people with the same problem to speak or write to the child to offer encouragement and support. Most 'stars' are very willing to do so.

3.10.3 Trichotillomania

Hair-pulling is an unusual problem which produces a condition similar to alopecia areata (see section 3.10.2). Hair-pullers often pluck out hair without relatives noticing and so the diagnosis is not always obvious. Close observation, however, reveals the cause. Rarely hair-pullers swallow their hair and the accumulation (*trichobezoar*) may cause intestinal obstruction. This self-damaging behaviour is, like other such behaviours, indicative of deeper difficulties.

Management involves behavioural approaches (Chapter 9) such as ignoring the hair-pulling, or teaching the child alternative and less harmful mannerisms, and rewarding hair growth on the bald patches. The underlying problem should be identified and treated.

3.10.4 Dermatitis artefacta

This is a rare condition in childhood in which the individual deliberately damages the skin by scratching or cutting it. The diagnosis is usually obvious, providing it is considered. The problem, as with other self-damaging behaviour such as anorexia nervosa or hair-pulling, reflects deeper difficulties which need to be recognized and resolved.

3.11 ABUSE SYNDROMES

3.11.1 Introduction

In a recent editorial 1987 was described as the Year of Child Abuse, with the category of crimes against children continuing and increasing—neglect, deprivation, emotional, physical and sexual abuse, Munchausen by proxy, child abduction, torture and murder having all been in the headlines (Lask, 1987a). In this section we describe the somatic presentations of these all too common problems. We recognize that abuse is a parental action rather than a subcategory of childhood disorder, but the effects of abuse undoubtedly fit well in this chapter.

3.11.2 Emotional abuse (including neglect and deprivation)

Emotional abuse has been defined as present in 'children under the age of 17 yrs whose behaviour and emotional development have been severely affected and where medical and social assessments find evidence of either persistent or severe neglect or rejection'. Over-protection and prevention from achieving normal independence may also be considered as forms of emotional abuse (Graham, 1986).

Whilst the features include severe emotional, behavioural and developmental problems, a common consequence is non-organic failure to thrive (see also section 3.6.2). A child who presents with miserable, apathetic and withdrawn behaviour, who is also failing to thrive, and in whom no organic disorder can be identified, should be considered to be suffering from emotional abuse until proved otherwise. Occasionally emotionally deprived children behave in an extrovert, disinhibited and almost 'promiscuous' manner, readily befriending and trusting anyone who will pay attention. Other somatic reactions to neglect include recurrent injuries and persistent physical ill health. There is often an overlap with physical abuse (see below).

Management of emotional abuse is highly complex and beyond the remit of this section. A multidisciplinary approach is essential, with careful consultation and liaison between all the professionals concerned. The failure to thrive should be treated as outlined in section 3.6.2. A decision must be made as to whether to attempt to reintegrate such children with their families, and how far to persist with such attempts, or whether alternative homes should be found.

The outcome for these children is varied. Up to 40% fail to achieve either normal weight or height. Many suffer physical abuse, and have persisting emotional and behavioural problems (Mrazek and Mrazek, 1985).

3.11.3 Physical abuse

Non-accidental injury of children is tragically common, and it is estimated that at least one child dies each day in Britain as a result of physical abuse, whilst in the USA the mortality rate is in excess of 2000 a year.

The presentation is enormously varied, including bites, bruises, eye and head injuries, broken limbs and burns. Between 4 and 8% of hospitalized burns patients have been abused (Mrazek and Mrazek, 1985). Failure to thrive in such children is common. Isolated incidents may not give rise to suspicion but recurrent episodes must cause concern. A direct report by a child that the injury was inflicted by someone else should always be believed until evidence to the contrary is available (Mrazek and Mrazek, 1985). If the parents cannot account for the injury, or give an implausible explanation, or have delayed seeking help, levels of suspicion should be high. The differential diagnosis, which is varied, complex and vital, is discussed in detail by Cooper (1978).

Management, as with emotional abuse, is beyond the remit of this section. A multidisciplinary approach is essential and clear decisions must be made with regard to placement of the child and attempts at rehabilitation of the family. Mrazek and Mrazek (1985) and Cooper (1978) provide helpful overviews.

Outcome—further abuse occurs in one-third of families in treatment, and unless clear changes have occurred in the family the risk of further abuse of the child and siblings is high. Abused children have persisting emotional and behavioural problems, and frequently become abusing parents.

3.11.4 Munchausen by proxy (fabricated illness)

This condition is characterized by maternal falsification of the medical histories of their children, leading to multiple and unnecessary and sometimes dangerous investigations (Meadow, 1982). The children, of any age up to early teens, present with a bizarre selection of serious signs and symptoms, often reflecting multisystem disorders. Alternatively there may be reports of only one symptom which is, however, fairly dramatic, for example loss of consciousness or haematuria for which no cause can be found. Most children have been seen by several doctors. In virtually every case so far reported the mother has been the perpetrator, without the father's knowledge. Either she has fabricated the symptom or has harmed the child by, for example, choking or poisoning. One diabetic mother substituted her own urine for that of her child, leading to repeated extensive investigations of glycosuria, whilst another contaminated her daughter's urine specimen with her own menstrual blood to support her complaint of haematuria.

Common features include: (1) persistent, recurrent inexplicable symptoms or illness; (2) investigation results inconsistent with the history and clinical findings; (3) an over-attentive mother who is unwilling to leave her child unattended by herself at any time, and who readily makes herself at home in hospital; (4) a mother who has herself had medical, nursing or pharmaceutical training, who is often able to predict when episodes are likely to occur, and whose husband is peripheral or totally absent. A recently described variant of this condition (Warner and Hathaway, 1984) involves mothers insisting that their children have severe allergies necessitating dramatic dietary restriction or other harmful measures (see also section 3.12).

Management is similar to that for emotional and physical abuse. Obtaining proof is often extremely difficult but is essential if progress is to be made. Toxicology screening at the time of episodes is helpful, and determined attempts should be made to observe the child in the mother's absence. Recently video cameras have been used (without the mother's knowledge) and have shown two mothers strangling their children, thus explaining the convulsion and loss of consciousness. Such an approach might be considered unethical, but it should be remembered that both children might otherwise have died. Doctors should be wary of making the situation worse by battering the child with further investigations when the problem is the parent's behaviour (Meadow, 1982).

Multiprofessional team work is required and legal matters have to be resolved. If the mother is unable to acknowledge her role, the outlook is bad, and the child should be removed from her care. If this is not possible for lack of evidence, every effort should be made to ensure close follow-up.

3.11.5 Child sexual abuse (CSA)

Before describing this problem in detail, a definition is required. No single definition of CSA is necessarily correct, for definitions vary depending on the reason for which it is required—medical, social, psychological or legal (Markowe, 1988). For the purposes of this section CSA may be described as the exposure of a child by an adult to a sexual experience, ranging from showing pornography, or indecent exposure, through to oral, vaginal or anal coitus. It is estimated that, using such a definition, up to one-third of all children may have been abused (Mrazek and Mrazek, 1985). If more stringent criteria are used, concentrated on actual sexual assault, 12% of a sample of 930 women reported at least one incidence of intrafamilial sexual experience before the age of 14, and 16% by the age of 18. In the same sample 20% reported at least one extrafamilial experience before age 14, and 31% by the age of 18 (Russell, 1983). Combining the figures and allowing for overlap, 25% of the respondents had had an uninvited sexual experience before they were 14 and 40% before 18. Nor should the frequency of the sexual abuse of boys be underestimated.

The somatic manifestations of CSA are considerable. Common presentations include vaginal bleeding or discharge, enuresis, recurrent urinary tract infections, proctitis or rectal bleeding, constipation or soiling, venereal disease, anorexia, food refusal, nausea or vomiting. A wide range of behavioural and emotional disturbances may accompany the physical symptoms, including overt sexualized behaviour such as masturbation, physical provocativeness and exhibitionism.

Management—detailed discussion is beyond the remit of this section. As with other forms of abuse a multidisciplinary approach is necessary, and any professional who discovers CSA is obliged to inform the appropriate authorities. Keeping it confidential is neither ethically nor legally acceptable, and is most certainly not in the child's interests, even when the child pleads for privacy. The roles and responsibilities of the different professionals involved, and ways of engaging the child, family and, if within the family, the alleged perpetrator, whilst at the same time ensuring the protection of the child and fulfilling responsibilities to society, are topics comprehensively discussed elsewhere (e.g., Mrazek and Kempe, 1981; Porter, 1984; Bentovim, 1987; Bentovim *et al.*, 1987b).

Outcome is difficult to determine given the problems of definition, diagnosis and follow-up. From a review of the literature Mrazek and Mrazek (1985) consider that the most consistent problems are of psychosexual adjustment, but educational difficulties and a wide range of emotional and behavioural disorders in the short and long term have been described.

3.12 SPECIFIC SYNDROMES

In this final section of the chapter we consider a group of disorders that have a number of similarities, in that they each have specific primary causes, and present with multiple different physical symptoms, for which no convincing biological cause can be found, creating considerable diagnostic confusion. These are (1) 'myalgic encephalopathy', (2) school refusal, and (3) high-achieving syndrome.

3.12.1 'Myalgic encephalopathy' (ME)

We put this title in inverted commas to indicate our doubts as to its validity. It refers to a group of patients (adults and children) who present with a history (often for several months, and sometimes years) of various complaints, most commonly fatigue, loss of energy, poor appetite, nausea and lowering of mood. Sometimes there are various pains, and occasionally weight loss. Children often present with a triad of symptoms—not eating, not walking and not talking. They claim to feel too unwell to eat or walk, and are remarkably uncommunicative.

Parents are convinced that there must be a physical cause as the symptoms often immediately post-date an undisputed viral infection. In other cases there is an absolute conviction that allergy must be responsible. Parents give a history of allergy and convincing accounts of allergic reactions.

Physical examination and investigations reveal no obvious current organic pathology, although various viral titres may be raised, indicating previous viral infection. Allergy is rarely discovered.

Management—once obvious physical disease has been excluded, searches for more obscure conditions should cease. Careful observation of the child's behaviour and mental state indicate an emotional disorder, which Professor Phillip Graham at Great Ormond Street (personal communication) has referred to as a different type of ME—'manipulative emotionality'. Characteristically such children seem to have a degree of control over their behaviour, and their 'illness' becomes a focus for family life, often distracting from other problems. In hospital they seem to make good relationships with other children and to behave more normally when not with adults. Their lowered mood and determined avoidance of eating, walking and talking reappears in the presence of adults. This observation distinguishes the condition from a true clinical depression, where such variation does not occur (Lask, 1988a). Psychosocial exploration almost always reveals family problems and sometimes school difficulties.

Using techniques described in succeeding chapters the parents are helped to recognize the true nature of the disorder. It sometimes helps to offer a diagnostic label such as 'post-viral depression' or even 'pseudo-allergy', which are more accurate a description than 'myalgic encephalopathy'. Whatever label is used it is important to clarify that psychosocial factors are now more important, although the condition may have been precipitated by a biological process. Further management is similar to that outlined in section 3.8.1 for psychogenic disorders of movement and sensation.

Outcome is dependent on the parents' ability to accept the correct diagnosis and to work on the underlying problems. Many children make a full recovery under these circumstances, but others, whose parents are unable to comply, may remain invalided for years.

3.12.2 School refusal ('masquerade syndrome')

Refusal to attend school is a well-documented problem, described as 'school refusal' or 'school phobia', and clearly differentiated from truancy (e.g., Hersov and Berg, 1980). 'School refusal' is a better term than 'school phobia', as in many instances the intense fear is not specifically about school but more generally about separation, and is akin to separation anxiety. In truancy there is no anxiety about school or separation, but rather a wilful absconding from school, with or without parental knowledge or approval, often associated with other forms of antisocial behaviour, and often in the company of peers.

Usually school refusal is readily recognizable because the child openly expresses major concerns about going to school, and may not have attended school for several weeks or months. A group of school refusers that is less easily recognized consists of children who present with intense physical symptoms, such as headache, abdominal pain, vomiting, limp or generalized fatigue and apathy. No organic cause can be found for their symptoms, and often it is only when a firm statement is made that the child should return to school, regardless of the symptoms, that the diagnosis becomes clear. At this point such children protest vehemently, insist that they are too unwell to attend, and may rage and scream. This is in contrast to children who are physically unwell for reasons other than anxiety about school attendance, including children with truly serious illnesses such as epilepsy, diabetes, asthma or bowel disease.

It is because of the hidden quality of the school refusal in these children that this condition is sometimes known as 'masquerade syndrome'. As with school refusal generally, it is most common in the 10–14-year age group, but occurs more often in girls than boys.

Management involves helping parents and child accept the true nature of the disorder, and attempting to understand and alleviate the associated anxieties. As such exploration may take a long time and the continuing absence from school reinforces the anxieties, it is wise to insist on a rapid return to school. It is pathognomonic that the child will violently resist this, threatening the most dire consequences if the planning proceeds. An immediate exacerbation or demonstration of symptoms frequently occurs.

The parents need to be advised that they must take charge and plan together how to organize the return to school, who is to liaise with the school, and how to support each other through what will be a very difficult time. Attempts to detour from this, by returning to the symptoms, invariably occur, with the parents and child all participating. It is useful to point this out, and separate discussion of the symptoms and their significance from the practical arrangements. It should be made clear that further help will be available after return to school, to consolidate the progress and overcome underlying problems. Frequently there is a marital problem, the difficulties of which have been ignored because of the child's 'illness'. Help can be offered for this should the parents wish. If the parents can accept the diagnosis and work together, resisting their child's protests and threats, there is almost always a successful return to school during the next few days. When this approach fails a more graded return to school may help, using the principles of graded desensitization (see Chapter 9).

Alternative techniques include the use of environmental manipulation, such as transferring the child to a smaller school with smaller classes, or to an educational facility specifically designed for children with fears of attending school. As a last resort hospitalization could be used as a base for returning to school, initially accompanied by nursing staff, and then by parents alone. Antidepressants should only be used for obvious depression and anxiolytic agents may help, if only as a face-saver. Beta-blockers such as propranolol (see Chapter 10) are useful when anxiety is somatized, as in this disorder.

3.12.3 High-achieving syndrome

In contrast to 'ME' and school refusal, this group of children, who also have mysterious and unexplained symptoms, are generally easy-going, contented and cooperative. Prior to their illness they have been 'perfect' children, good at everything, well behaved, a pleasure to have around, top of their class, very popular, and successfully involved in many activities (Lask, 1986). They regularly win prizes and awards. The families tend to be happy and well functioning, characterized by warmth, mutual care and consideration, and altruism. With reference to the sick child they say 'we only ask that she does her best'.

The illness starts, as in the 'ME' group, with a mild injury or viral infection but fails to resolve. Physical examination and investigation reveal insignificant non-specific findings. Superficial psychiatric assessment is unhelpful, for such children appear to be perfectly well adjusted. Only by patient and subtle probing is a picture obtained of a child who cannot bear to fail, and who would never criticize her parents or express negative feelings. Such children tend to be aged 10–14 and are far more often girls.

These girls are in an intolerable situation for, being genetically well endowed and with a happy family background, they have become high-achievers. They share with their families high expectations of themselves. They persist in doing their best and allow no respite, socially or academically. Ultimately a minor sports injury or viral infection allows a way out. Unrecognized stress delays or prevents recovery, and the subsequent easing of pressure reinforces the status quo of ill health. These children characteristically make little fuss and willingly attempt to attend school.

Variations on this theme include children with one particular but exceptional talent, be it in sports, the arts or an academic subject (Lask, 1988b). The pressure to utilize this talent to the full, with consequent intensive training, studying or practising, and isolation from peers, gradually erodes the child's sense of well-being and provides a fertile breeding ground for an intercurrent illness to take root.

Management involves explaining to the parents the nature of the symptoms, and it is startling how readily they can accept such an interpretation. This is in contrast to many more disturbed families who totally reject a psychological explanation (see Chapter 6). The parents are helped to convince their children that imperfection is acceptable and that occasional failure does not matter. They are asked to define what they mean by 'do your best', to quantify it, and to prescribe 'off days'. The children are told that anxiety, anger and sadness are all normal, healthy feelings that everyone experiences and needs to express. The family are helped to communicate and share distress rather than denying our detouring it (see Chapter 8).

Outcome is usually very satisfactory, for such families are always willing to work on difficulties and use advice that is offered. High standards and good performance persist but not at such a high pitch and not at the cost of poor health.

3.13 SUMMARY

Stress and distress can produce virtually any physical symptoms, and the physician should certainly not discount psychological factors as a possible cause, whatever the symptoms. The true diagnosis can be difficult to elicit when the symptoms appear convincingly physical. However, there must be a point when physical investigations should cease.

CHAPTER 4

The Illness Network

Humpty Dumpty sat on a wall
Humpty Dumpty had a great fall
All the King's horses and all the King's men
Couldn't put Humpty together again

GUIDE FOR THE READER

It has always been a mystery why the King's crack troops couldn't repair
Humpty Dumpty. Indeed, it is not at all clear how Humpty met his accident.
Did he slip, was he pushed, or did he jump? Certainly the King was wise to
adopt a team approach to such a complex and intractable problem, but were
they deployed in such a way that they were able to consider every aspect? Did
Humpty comply with treatment? Were his parents involved or were they
tackling the problem independently? And did the troops seek further information about Humpty's past history and family background, not to mention his
school performance? We do not know what predisposed Humpty to such a
dilemma, what precipitated it, or what perpetuated it. For a successful resolution, we would need to understand and involve this wide network.

4.1 INTRODUCTION

There is a complex series of interactions between the child, his illness, the
family and extrafamilial factors (Figure 4.1). We propose to call this the 'illness
network'. In this chapter we consider in detail the structure and clinical
relevance of the interaction between illness and each of the other components of
the network. In so doing we make an artificial distinction between the components. For example, in considering specifically the relationship between the
child and the illness there is the possibility of appearing to neglect the influence
of the family. However, Figure 4.1 demonstrates clearly that whatever happens
in one interaction affects each of the others.

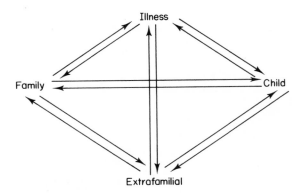

Figure 4.1 Illness network

4.2 ILLNESS AND THE CHILD

4.2.1 The psychosocial consequences of illness

Responses to illness can be handicapping, and sometimes more so than the illness itself. We need therefore to give careful consideration to the common responses, both optimal and detrimental (Cadman *et al.*, 1987). Illness permeates all spheres of a child's life—physical, social and psychological. Factors that influence adjustment include the type of illness, attributes of the child such as age of onset, temperament and intelligence, and family characteristics such as their attitude to the illness, communication patterns and quality of parenting.

Recognizing the effects of the illness is important not simply because to do so is humane and reasonable. Adverse consequences can play a key role in perpetuating or aggravating the illness whilst, in contrast, optimal coping is likely to lead to better health care and outcome. Figure 4.2 illustrates some possible interactions between the illness and its consequences.

Let us consider, for example, a 13-year-old boy with diabetes. The illness may cause him to feel tired or sick, whilst the fluctuation in blood sugar levels may lead to some visual focusing difficulties. These dysfunctional physiological processes render the child apathetic and dispirited. Equally, he may be aware of the possibility of serious complications as the years go by, and become angry and resentful. These psychosocial consequences (apathy, anxiety, despair, resentment) can have an adverse effect on the illness itself, via one or both pathways (Figure 4.2). Emotional arousal may directly influence glucose metabolism by increasing levels of free fatty acid (Minuchin *et al.*, 1978). Alternatively, the boy's resentment or apathy may lead to poor compliance with diet or medication. Thus a vicious cycle may be initiated or maintained, incorporating up to four possible pathways.

Figure 4.2 Illness and its consequences

Similar sequences can be observed in many different illnesses. A 10-year-old girl with cystic fibrosis was rendered depressed, angry, resentful and helpless by her physical limitations, breathlessness and awareness of the severity of her illness. She adamantly refused to have her frequent sessions of physiotherapy, whilst the associated depression led to a marked loss of appetite and subsequent weight loss. Each pathway indicated in Figure 4.2 was operative.

Fritz (1987) has demonstrated the tragic significance of psychosocial responses to illness in a study of factors in fatal childhood asthma. Depression, denial, emotional triggers for attacks, and unsupportive families were found to be frequent concomitants when children died from asthma.

Given the crucial significance of psychosocial consequences we need to give some thought to what factors are relevant in determining responses.

4.2.2 Major determining factors

4.2.2.1 Type of illness

Illness may be mild or severe, localized or general, acute or chronic, and relapsing or unremitting. Using extremes as examples, a child with a mild, localized, short-lived problem such as migraine is, in general, likely to cope better than another child with a severe, generalized, long-lasting and unremitting disorder such as chronic renal disease. It is perfectly possible, however, for the former child to react adversely if, for example, the parental response is one of over-involvement, over-protectiveness and extreme anxiety.

4.2.2.2 Illness-imposed constraints

These may have a powerful adverse effect by defining the child as different from friends. This becomes particularly relevant in adolescence, when peer relationships are so central. The inability to play in a school team, for example, may set apart such children, compromise their self-image, and lead to such reactions as denial, non-compliance and depression.

4.2.2.3 Age of onset

This influences the impact in several ways. Any recently achieved milestone, such as being dry at night, or just starting school, are likely casualties of the associated regression (see section 4.2.5). Necessary medical procedures may aggravate age-determined common fears. For example, the monitoring and treatment of recent-onset diabetes in a 6-year-old, when fear of needles is common, becomes particularly complicated.

Children's conceptions of illness, death and how their bodies work mature as they grow older. For example, a 6-year-old may assume that her illness is a punishment for an assumed wrong-doing, or that she might pass it on to a parent by cuddling. Either of these false assumptions may lead to unnecessary distress. The different phases of conceptualization and their clinical implications are discussed by Bibace and Walsh (1981).

4.2.2.4 Temperament

A particular cluster of temperaments (irregularity of biological function, non-adaptability to change, predominantly negative responses to new stimuli, intense reactions and distractibility) makes adaptation to the intrusion of disease more difficult (Thomas *et al.*, 1968). The necessary changes in daily routine may be met with anger, resistance and age-determined signs of distress (see section 4.2.5). More adaptable children fare better.

4.2.2.5 Intelligence

This influences responses to illness in a similar manner to age-related conceptualizations (see above). In the general population, childhood adjustment problems are inversely correlated with intelligence (Rutter *et al.*, 1970). When ill, brighter children are better able to devise strategies to enable them to cope more successfully.

In the next section we distinguish, somewhat artificially, between attitudinal, emotional, behavioural and somatic responses.

4.2.3 Attitudinal responses

Attitudes vary along a continuum from over-acceptance of the illness to complete denial. Figure 4.3 represents this spectrum as a balance-beam and fulcrum, for it is not uncommon for children (and their families) to fluctuate between the extremes. Optimal realistic acceptance lies midway. A fixed position at either extreme, or continuous fluctuations, create many problems.

Over-acceptance is manifested by an excessive preoccupation with the illness, high levels of anxiety, and a tendency to allow the illness to take over. Such children usually have parents who adopt a similar attitude (see Chapter 8). This is an understandable (and not abnormal) initial reaction to the onset of illness, but should usually be short-lived.

Bobby, aged 10, had suffered from asthma for six years. He was addicted to his inhaler, fearful of going out alone, and as soon as he started coughing or wheezing would notify his mother, or ask his teacher if he could go home. He would not participate in any physical activity, although his respiratory function tests often showed minimal impairment, even after exercise. He rarely visited friends. His mother reinforced his behaviour from the onset of the illness by reacting vigorously to even the slightest of symptoms.

Over-acceptance   Denial

Figure 4.3 Attitude spectrum

Denial, in contrast, is manifested by the tendency to play down the problem, disregard symptoms, and disclaim the severity (or even the very presence) of the disease. Again such children tend to have parents who adopt the same attitude.

Another 10-year-old with asthma, Julie, refused to accept the limitations imposed by her illness, and the necessity for regular medication. She always attempted to join in any physical activities at school, and ignored completely warning signals of exacerbations of the asthma. In consequence she was frequently admitted to hospital with severe respiratory impairment. Her mother and stepfather never encouraged or even reminded her to take her medication. Her father had died from asthma, and the family attitude was that drawing attention to the illness would reinforce it.

Another attitudinal response linked to the above spectrum is that relating to *generalization* of the handicap. A child may correctly experience the problem as limited and circumscribed, or incorrectly as globally handicapping. For example, diabetic children may perceive themselves as generally well, except for some cells in the pancreas that are not working, or as generally debilitated—'ill all over'. Thus the first child might say 'there are few things that I can't do',

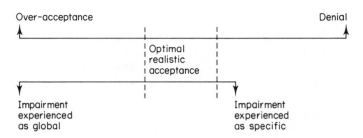

Figure 4.4 Attitudes and perception of impairment

whilst the other would say 'I am a handicapped person and I can't really do anything properly'.

Figure 4.4 illustrates the relationship between the attitude spectrum on the one hand, and the impairment spectrum on the other.

4.2.4 Emotional responses

Illness inevitably gives rise to a wide range of powerful feelings. The more serious the illness and the longer it lasts, the more relevant and intense become such reactions. In addition important longitudinal changes occur during a lengthy illness. The shifts are clinically important because they can impair the effectiveness of medical interventions (see Figure 4.2). Although exceptions are common, the timing, quality and manifestation of emotional responses show recognizable patterns. It is clinically useful to anticipate these changes with some families early in the course of the illness. Such reactions affect to a variable degree all family members (see section 4.3.1).

4.2.4.1 Initial emotional responses

Initial emotional responses to the onset of a serious illness resemble (but show important differences from) patterns typical of grief reactions associated with a major loss, such as death of a loved one: i.e. shock, denial, sadness, anger, adjustment. Figure 4.5 illustrates the phasic nature of such responses—transient shock, early denial that gradually fades in the face of reality, and sadness mixed with anger. The pattern may repeat itself when the illness is relapsing and remitting, as in cases of asthma or leukaemia. The illustration portrays a typical reaction but many variations can occur.

Shock is a brief period of intense emotional arousal following the disclosure of an extremely distressing piece of news. It tends to last at most for a few days and is soon replaced by denial.

Denial is manifested by an inability to accept the severity of the illness and the belief that a mistake has been made, or that all will work out well. Although

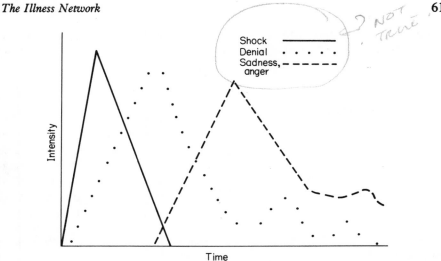

Figure 4.5 Initial reactions to serious illness

denial is often a short-lived phase, it may return in some form at times of disease remission or quiescence. In some extreme instances denial persists indefinitely (see Chapter 3). Such reactions are associated with little motivation to learn the treatment regimen, and poor compliance with any restrictions in diet, autonomy or peer relationships.

Sadness and anger, like shock and denial, are normal, healthy responses to chronic ill health. They vary in intensity and length, but a fluctuating course is to be expected. Sadness elicits more empathy and comforting behaviour than anger, although supportive responses would be more appropriate and helpful in both instances. Sadness may deepen to depression, especially when a parent is unable to cope. Frequent crying for no obvious reason, withdrawal, inactivity, poor appetite, irritability and sleep problems are all indicators that depression is complicating the clinical picture.

4.2.4.2 *Changes in emotional responses with time*

A temporal pattern of shifting effect is commonly seen in children with chronic illness. The swings tend to be amplified or attenuated by the natural course of the disease. As the illness responds to treatment or begins to remit, relief becomes the dominant emotion. In the process of discovering the return of previous abilities, a degree of denial returns. This state of relative happiness and enhanced self-esteem may be slowly tempered as disease-imposed limits are encountered. In a relatively static phase, these limits will be stable, and once more the child may learn to cope and experience a subsequent lifting of mood.

With prolonged or increasing loss of abilities, the phasic pattern of emotional responses persists. In relapsing illness this cycle is prominent but the magnitude of mood swings tends to diminish as time goes by.

4.2.4.3 Expression of emotions

The recognition, acceptance and discussion of a sick child's feelings is an important aspect of helping that child towards an optimal adjustment. The child's mode of emotional expression is determined by such factors as temperament, personality and family responses (see Chapter 3). In families who tend to internalize (bottle up) emotions, the children are likely to adopt the same style. In consequence anger and sadness may not be expressed overtly, and may therefore not be recognized and alleviated. This may lead to an intolerable intensification of such feelings, with ensuing depression or exacerbation of ill health. Children from families who can tolerate the expression of painful feelings are much more likely to be able to do so themselves.

Sometimes a child may not be fully aware himself of these feelings, and it is then a much more difficult and skilled task to help him get in touch with his emotions as well as to express them (see Chapter 9).

4.2.4.4 Fantasies

Conceptualization of disease in healthy children is age-dependent. Five- to 6-year-olds consider illness to have magical causes or to be a consequence of some transgression. By 9–10 years the presence of germs is taken as sufficient to cause disease. By 12–13 years children are able to understand that illness may be caused by combinations of factors (Perrin and Gerrity, 1981). However, illness causes regression and therefore ill children are likely to be utilizing more primitive concepts than their age would suggest. The active concept of disease causation often becomes integrated with two other primitive concepts, i.e. omnipotence and magical thinking. Children use a mixture of these ideas to speculate about questions of cause and prognosis.

In situations of serious illness even adolescents can entertain the idea that their illness is a punishment for misbehaviour or being a bad person. Occasionally they are worried that they have physically injured someone by being angry with them, and their own illness is a reprisal. Such fantasies are a confusion about disease causation linked to age-related conceptual errors, or to regression. Whenever possible, ill children's fantasies about the cause and effect of their illness should be elicited and replaced with the, usually, less frightening reality.

Figure 4.6 illustrates the distressing fantasies of a child aged 8, Asif, who had suffered from nephrotic syndrome from the age of 1 to 5, necessitating complex treatment including nasogastric feeding. He was referred for psychiatric help

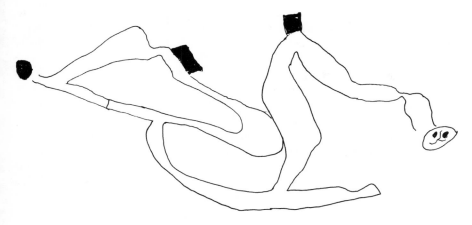

Figure 4.6 Asif's drawing

because of his refusal to eat, and insistence that he be fed through a nasogastric tube.

He describes his drawing as follows:

> It's about me; that's me at the side and I have to go along this tube, and straight away it goes very narrow and may strangle me. That blotch is a monster who may catch me, but if I get past him there's a sort of crossroads, and I don't known which way to go. If I go the wrong way I get stuck, and if I go the right way, there's another sort of crossroads. I might get stuck again and I might meet Godzilla, who's that black square. If he likes you he looks after you but if he doesn't he kills you. And even if I get to the end of the tube there's a large black hole that swallows you up.'

Asif had integrated the nasogastric tube into his fantasy world, and was able to describe vividly all the dangers. Most significantly, he appeared to indicate that by separating from the tube he would die. A series of discussions helping him to separate fantasy from reality, combined with a desensitization programme (see Chapter 7) enabled him to overcome his dependence on the tube, and eat normally.

Children's fantasies are often determined by and interwoven with myths about illness (see Chapter 8).

4.2.5 Behavioural responses

The type of behavioural response is to some extent age-determined. In infancy, crying and feeding disturbances are common; toddlers manifest increased activity, sleep and feeding problems; in the pre-school group toileting difficulties join the list; in school-age children behavioural problems and poor academic performance might be expected, whilst adolescents are likely to be even more difficult than usual, fail to comply with treatment, perform poorly in school, and have peer group problems.

At any age, *regression* commonly occurs as a response to illness. Even most adults have an emotional as well as a physical need to be looked after when unwell. The wish to curl up in a warm place with a comforting object such as a hot-water bottle, a good book or a cuddly toy is a universal response to illness. The emotional regression is accompanied by a behavioural regression. Children may lose skills recently acquired, such as dryness at night, and in general revert to an earlier stage of functioning. For most this is a temporary phenomenon. Nonetheless, because it elicits comforting and privileges from parents, many children attempt to prolong the situation. Parents who persistently concede to such demands, once they have become inappropriate, reinforce the regressed behaviour, and may ultimately come to regret their over-acquiescence.

Nonetheless, it is important to allow children an initial and natural regression during illness. Ultimately they must work towards an optimal realistic acceptance of the problem, whatever the constraints, intensity and length of the illness (see Figure 4.3).

4.2.6 Somatic responses

Somatic responses to the anxiety associated with ill health are virtually inevitable. The discomfort and distress of illness leads to high levels of emotional arousal, with a heightened physical awareness and sensitivity. Each symptom, be it difficulty with movement, pain or breathlessness, may be exacerbated by the associated distress. Any other physiologically vulnerable organ or body system may respond to emotional triggers. For example, a child who has a predisposition to recurrent abdominal pain (see Chapter 3) is likely to suffer exacerbations as a consequence of an unrelated condition, such as recurrent urinary infection. Even distant pathology such as injury to a limb can have the same effect.

4.3 ILLNESS AND THE FAMILY

The reader will not be surprised that we start this section by emphasizing the *interaction* between illness and the family. No one would dispute that illness can affect the family, but all to often it is forgotten that family dysfunction can trigger illness. For example, a child caught up in marital conflict, with each parent trying to get him to take sides, will eventually develop a problem, the nature of which will be determined by his temperament and physiological predisposition. The problem will in turn affect the marital disharmony, which itself further influences the problem, and so on. Ultimately the balance of forces settles into a homeostasis—i.e. disturbance of one part of the family affects the whole, and sets in motion compensatory events to re-establish equilibrium (Lask, 1982b, 1987b). Figure 4.7 illustrates this sequence in its simplest form.

Figure 4.7 Illness and family functioning

4.3.1 The effect of illness on the family

Illness has a variety of effects on the family. For example, Reddihough and her colleagues (1977) found that the families of asthmatic colleagues had basic misconceptions about the illness and its therapy, and intense fears about death and damage to the heart and lungs, and that the disease placed a burden— emotional, financial and practical—on all family members, and especially on the mother. Similar findings have been reported for other illnesses, for example diabetes and epilepsy (Lask, 1988c). Siblings are often adversely affected psychologically, sometimes even more than the sick child. Neglect of the sibling and over-protection of the 'patient' is a common pattern. Psychiatric morbidity is higher in the parents with children with chronic illness than parents of normal children. For some unhappy or disturbed parents the illness becomes their *raison d'être*. This is an extreme example of parental over-involvement, the opposite pole being complete denial of the severity of (or in rare cases even the existence of) the illness. The over-involvement–denial attitude spectrum in parents is mirrored by that in children. This is discussed further in Chapter 8.

4.3.2 The effect of the family on the illness

As mentioned earlier, family dysfunction can cause or aggravate ill health. Detailed descriptions of this process are available elsewhere (Minuchin *et al.*, 1978; Lask, 1982b). There is no evidence for the view that specific family constellations create specific family illnesses. What is more likely is that the stresses associated with living with a dysfunctional family trigger the physio- logically vulnerable organ or system (see Chapter 2), with subsequent ill health.

Families play a vital part in the management of any illness. Ample evidence exists to show that certain key factors are associated with a better prognosis (Lask, 1988b). These include a good marriage, an optimal realistic attitude, satisfactory adaptation, stability, warmth, cohesion and satisfactory parental communication. Poor outcome is associated with marital disharmony, rigid or disorganized families, over-protective or denying families, and dysfunctional communication. This topic is discussed further, with case illustrations, in Chapter 8.

4.4 ILLNESS AND THE OUTSIDE WORLD

Figure 4.8 illustrates the quantity and complexity of the relationships surrounding a child's illness. (We are grateful to Dr Sheila Shribman for introducing us to her 'confusogram'.)

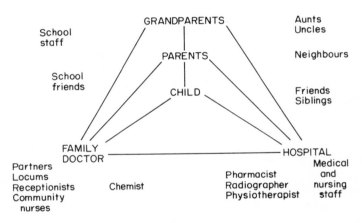

Figure 4.8 Shribman's confusogram

   In the earlier sections of this chapter we discussed the relationships between the child, the family and the illness. A large number of others are also involved in similar interactions. Some of these are portrayed in Figure 4.8. The potential for miscommunication, extreme attitudes and high levels of emotional arousal should not be underestimated! Perhaps what is most important for readers in relation to any particular child and family, is to consider their own role, attitude, quality of communication, consistency of management, and degree of warmth and empathy. Whilst to be perfect would be impossible, weaknesses or failings such as miscommunications, inconsistencies, extremes of attitude or a lack of warmth and empathy are likely to have an adverse effect on the course of the illness. We need only recall how important the doctor, nurse or other professionals become when we or our children are ill, for us to realize what a positive (or negative) influence health professionals can have on the course of a disorder.

4.5 SUMMARY

The illness network consists of a number of interdependent and interacting variables; the child, his illness, the family and the outside world. When this network functions well, the course of the illness is more likely to run smoothly. The converse also applies. Two examples illustrate this.

Rowan, aged 9, had been admitted to hospital 22 times in three years because of unstable diabetes. His parents argued endlessly about how to manage his diet, and his mother became grossly over-involved, allowing him no independence whatsoever. The family doctor felt she could not help any further, and the paediatrician desperately tried to separate Rowan and his mother. The school refused to have him in class because of his frequent hypoglycaemic episodes. The family resented referral to a psychiatrist and refused to accept any of his suggestions. The paternal grandparents paid for a consultation from an international expert on diabetes, who recommended a change of treatment regime. This had no effect, and the paediatrician became increasingly exasperated with the parents' failure to comply. They transferred to another doctor, but by the age of 11 Rowan had been admitted to hospital on 13 more occasions.

Alex was 10 when he received an ileostomy for his intractable Crohn's disease. His parents, encouraged by the medical and nursing staff, learned within three days how to change the ileostomy equipment, and taught him to do it for himself by the end of the first week. They helped him to return to school by devising with him a plan of what to say to other children, and how to cope in the showers and changing rooms. The school staff ensured that Alex was coping all right and nominated a teacher to whom he could go should there be any problems. Alex had no difficulties in settling back to a normal way of life, and remained in excellent health. At follow-up, aged 16 years, he was asked how he managed when he started dating. 'Well when I told my first girl-friend, she gave me a funny look, and wouldn't see me again. With my next one, we were just cuddling, and she felt the bag and asked what it was, and I told her, and she said "Oh" and we just carried on. It was great!'

In the next chapter we describe how to integrate all of the different components into the assessment process.

CHAPTER 5

A Psychosomatic Approach to Assessment

Children are too important to be the monopoly of doctors (Apley, 1971)

GUIDE FOR THE READER

As Apley implies, childhood disorder is too often the preserve of the medical profession. In this chapter we emphasize the importance of assessing *all* aspects of a problem—physical, developmental, social and psychological. The reader's professional training may determine priorities, but a truly psychosomatic approach considers each component to be of considerable importance. We describe in detail the diagnostic process, and demonstrate the value of making a formulation using a multi-axial diagnostic scheme.

5.1 INTRODUCTION

A psychosomatic (or comprehensive) assessment involves paying attention to physical, developmental, psychological and social aspects of the problem. Ideally each of these components is considered in parallel, rather than first dealing with the physical, then moving on to psychosocial features. A guaranteed way of ensuring that a referral to a psychologist or psychiatrist will fail is to tell the parents after a long list of investigations have excluded organic disease that 'We'd better see what the psychiatrist can find'.

The physician uses experience and judgement to determine exactly how much physical investigation is required. It is often difficult to know 'when to stop'. Meadow (1982), although discussing Munchausen by proxy, has some cautionary words that are relevant in many different circumstances:

> It was the doctors who injured the child most. Doctors behave in stereotyped ways and a symptom or sign is matched by an investigation or treatment. We still behave as if missing an organic cause for a complaint is the greatest sin. It is not. It is far worse to batter a child to near death with investigations and treatment when the

problem is the parent's behaviour. We should develop broader shoulders on which to bear the knowledge that we might miss some organic diagnoses, learn to tolerate uncertainty and unresolved problems, and remember the vista of behavioural variation.

Ideally, physical and psychosocial assessment start at the same time, at the first meeting. Usually the emphasis is on the physical aspects, but it is perfectly in order to state that almost always physical symptoms have a psychological effect, and very often a psychological cause, so that it is important to consider both sides. Experienced practitioners develop their own routine for introducing a comprehensive approach to assessment and treatment, the essential component of which is to make it clear at the start that body and mind are inseparable, and need therefore to be considered together.

Figure 5.1 portrays the relationships between the biological, social and psychological components of any childhood problem. The biological predisposition refers to the genetic factors and any physiological vulnerability, whilst the mediating mechanisms include causative agents. Thus if the illness is asthma, the biological predisposition is the inheritance of a labile bronchus, which readily goes into spasm when exposed to such triggers as infection, allergens, exercise or stress.

The quality of family functioning, such as adaptability, parental effectiveness, clarity of communication and ability to complete essential tasks such as decision making, problem solving and conflict resolution, plays an important part in determining the child's reaction to stress and illness. Similarly the child's psychological make-up, including temperament, personality, intelligence, adaptability and early life experiences, are all influential. Social factors that also require consideration include school performance, peer group relationships and communal support. Not all physicians would wish, or feel competent, to make a formal psychosocial assessment themselves, whilst non-physicians are clearly

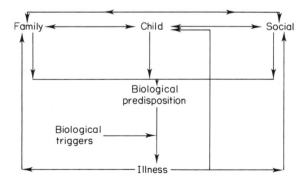

Figure 5.1 Illness cycle

not in a position to carry out physical assessments. In consequence, in describing in detail the psychosocial assessment we have made an artificial distinction between the two. The principles of the consultation are, however, applicable to any setting for any professional.

5.2 THE DIAGNOSTIC PROCESS

A successful assessment is dependent upon the interviewer being clearly in charge of the session, using a suitable room and materials, and with a plan of action. Time constraints can impede such consultations and it is wise to allow at least an hour, and preferably longer, for the meeting. Attempts should be made to see, at the very least, both parents or parental substitutes plus the child. However, a full assessment can only be achieved by seeing the whole family with whom the child lives. In later meetings it may also be helpful to meet grandparents or other close and significant relatives, even if they live elsewhere.

The room should afford a measure of privacy and ample space for enough chairs, arranged in a circle. Adequate age-appropriate drawing and play material should always be available and offered to the children.

We discuss the components of the diagnostic assessment as follows: (1) facilitation; (2) getting to know the family; (3) orientation; (4) eliciting the family's view of the problem; (5) observation techniques; (6) assessment of the family; (7) assessment of the child; (8) psychological assessment; (9) interviewer's reactions; and (10) additional sources of information.

5.2.1 Facilitation

Inevitably, the family will feel anxious and possibly defensive, and a successful interview is more likely if they can be put at ease. This may be done by discussing non-threatening topics such as the trip to the clinic, travel difficulties and so on. It may need only a minute or two to complete, although some families will take longer to feel comfortable. This and the next phase may well overlap or occur in reverse order.

5.2.2 Getting to know the family

The interviewer should introduce herself or himself, and then go round each person in turn, asking their names and ages. It helps to put children at their ease if they are asked a little about themselves, such as the name of their school, their hobbies or interests. Few children can resist an enthusiastic comment about their clothing or appearance such as 'I do like your sweatshirt' or 'What does the slogan/logo mean?' A relaxed and warm attitude at this stage is likely to lead to a far more useful interview.

5.2.3 Orientation

The interviewer at this stage explains to the family how the session will proceed, how long it will last and introduces any special features of the room such as one-way mirrors and audio-visual equipment.

5.2.4 Eliciting the family's view of the problem

By this stage some families will have already launched into an account of the problem. If not, however, the interviewer may invite the family to express their concerns. Frequently a parent will quickly respond, but sometimes there will be a discussion as to who should start, or the interviewer is asked who it should be. A useful response to this question is 'Whoever wants to'. Either way the manner in which the family respond to the invitation gives useful information about family functioning, as does most of what happens during the interview. Ideally each person in turn eventually has his say, either spontaneously or by invitation.

5.2.5 Observation techniques

What the family report to be the problem might differ considerably from observations made. This is not necessarily the contradiction it appears, but rather two parts of a whole. The family's view represents the parts of their experience of the situation that are within their consciousness. The interviewer's observations are more organized around the processes of interaction in the family—the repetitive sequences usually beyond their immediate awareness—and patterns and meanings of communication (see below).

For example, a family might report that their 10-year-old son gets headaches for no reason, whereas an observer might notice that he complains of a headache when his parents start arguing. A more common example might be of a family who deny any problems in their relationships, but whose positioning, posture and non-verbal communications present a different picture.

The information obtained from observation is just as important as the family's report. Immediately adjacent seating, similarity in posture and frequent touching often indicate very close relationships, whilst physical distance, avoidance of eye contact or touching, or an adversarial posture indicate detachment and hostility.

5.2.5.1 Levels of communication

Any communication contains at least three levels or aspects—content, control and effect. In general, conscious attention is captured or dominated by only one level, although each level is usually significant. Usually we are readily aware of the content of a communication such as 'I feel sick'. The associated affect may only be noticed if it is strongly expressed, for example as fear or anxiety. The control element of the communication may not be noticed at all. Yet the child who frequently reports to his parents, as he is getting ready for school, that he feels sick is communicating at three different levels—the manifest content, the fear of going to school, and the attempt to avoid school.

The effect and control aspects of communication may be explicit or covert. When a mother suggests that a doctor carry out further investigations because she is worried something has been missed, her effect and her attempt to control are explicit. If, however, she makes the same request but omits to state her worry, her affective element is covert, and the control overt. If the same mother states that her previous doctor always did a blood test and X-ray whenever these symptoms occurred, it may not be immediately obvious that she is attempting to control the doctor, who may be more preoccupied with whether or not such a request is appropriate.

Similar processes occur in other contexts. A father may say to a non-medical consultant that 'our doctor sent us to you just to be thorough and to check out everything, but he's fairly sure that she has got abdominal migraine. She's not the worrying type, we're a very happy family with no problems; and it's obvious that she's got a food allergy'. The father is covertly expressing resentment, and perhaps shame or guilt, and is attempting to control the outcome of the consultation.

These different levels of communication constitute a significant aspect of family interaction and are discussed in more detail in Chapter 8.

5.2.6 Assessment of family

As the interview progresses, information about how the family functions is gathered, both by report and observation. The interviewer will want to know about family strengths and weaknesses, and in particular about the quality of parenting, style of communication, and degrees of closeness and separateness. Information will also be gathered on the family's ability to make decisions, complete tasks, solve problems and resolve conflicts, and about whether they can express and respond appropriately to everyday needs and emotions. Such information is obtained by direct questioning and observation. It is often helpful also to ask families to discuss together particular issues, thus allowing the interviewer to observe family interaction. These aspects of family functioning are more fully discussed in Chapter 8.

5.2.7 Assessment of the child

This can be carried out during the course of the interview, or separately with the child alone. There are no rules as to which strategy is better. Some children are easier to interview alone, whilst others would find this too threatening. Valuable information can be obtained about the child simply by watching during the family interview. Full assessment includes observation on appearance, size, behaviour, capacity to relate, degree of activity, attention span, mood, thought content and process, perceptions, self-esteem, sexual identity, intelligence, development, play, drawings and fantasies. Obviously all of this information cannot be obtained in one interview, and in Chapter 9 we discuss in more detail methods of communicating with children.

5.2.8 Psychological assessment

A particularly important aspect of the child's assessment, all too frequently overlooked, is that of intellectual and developmental status. Children with intellectual and developmental delay, or specific learning difficulties, are very likely to have associated adjustment problems. The probability is even greater when the delay or difficulty has been previously unrecognized.

For example Alan, aged 10, made repeated complaints of headaches and dizzy spells. Physical examination and eye-testing revealed no abnormalities. His mother was convinced that he had some serious disease, whilst his stepfather thought he was malingering. A paediatrician added further physical investigations, all of which proved negative, and he attempted to reassure the mother. She was dissatisfied and finally insisted on a further paediatric opinion. The second paediatrician took a much broader approach to assessment and asked for a school report, which stated that Alan had considerable difficulty reading and that his spelling was appalling (this information could have been obtained at the initial consultation by the family practitioner). Psychometric testing by a psychologist revealed that Alan had a specific reading difficulty which caused him considerable distress in class, with mocking by peers. Remedial help enabled him to gradually overcome the problem and read at an age-appropriate level.

A rough assessment of intelligence, developmental level and reading skills should be made as part of any comprehensive assessment by whoever sees the child in the first instance. Referral to a psychologist for formal intelligence testing and assessment of developmental level, skills and ability should always be considered when a child presents with symptoms for which no other satisfactory explanation can be found.

Psychologists have at their disposal a battery of tests for obtaining information about many different aspects of psychological functioning. The main areas of assessment are:

Intelligence testing—there are many tests available, and amongst the most familiar are the WISC (R) (Wechsler, 1976) for children over 6, and the Merrill-Palmer (Stutsman, 1948) for younger children.
Reading attainment—amongst the most commonly used tests are the Neale

Analysis of Reading Ability (Neale, 1956) and the Schonell Test of Graded Word Ability (Schonell and Schonell, 1958).

Language ability—there is a vast array of tests, including the Developmental Language Scales (Reynell, 1969), for the assessment of receptive and expressive language ability in younger children, the Utah (Mecham *et al.*, 1967), an overall measure of langauge which can be used for any age up to 15, and the Lowe and Costello (1976), which measures symbolic play, and therefore receptive language in the pre-school group.

Projective testing—this technique purports to elicit unconscious ideas and feelings, and other aspects of personality; considerable controversy surrounds the validity and reliability of such tests, which include the Rorschach (1942) and the Thematic Apperception Test (Murray, 1938).

Repertory grids are a form of personality map based on personal construct theory, most clearly explained by Bannister and Fransella (1971).

A fuller discussion of psychological assessment and testing is to be found in a paper by Berger (1985), and a detailed review of the tests available for assessing speech and language in a paper by Cantwell and Baker (1985).

5.2.9 Interviewer's reactions

The relationship the family establishes with the interviewer, and the way that family members relate to each other during the consultation, will trigger emotional responses in the interviewer. Most practitioners in the caring professions are not cognitively aware of these emotions unless they are very strongly felt. In such instances the professional complains to peers about the difficult family or acts on feelings without analysing them. Psychotherapists generally call these feelings counter-transference and attempt to allow for or utilize them in therapy. Indeed, these feelings can be a rich source of information about the emotional responses individual family members generate in each other and about the emotional milieu of the family. The feelings are also a sample of the emotions the family evokes when dealing with people outside the family.

In practice the interviewer's emotional responses are as important a piece of information as aspects of the history of the problem or special investigations such as an X-ray or an IQ test, and can be usefully incorporated into the assessment.

Adam, aged 9, suffered bouts of recurrent chest pain. During the diagnostic assessment his father dominated the interview, criticized his wife and children and repeatedly challenged the interviewer. The other family members avoided eye-contact and made no spontaneous contributions. The emotional atmosphere as experienced by the interviewer was tense and unpleasant, and gave clues as to the genesis of Adam's chest pain.

5.2.10 Additional sources of information

Teachers, other professionals and extended family members are the most frequent sources of additional social information (see Figure 5.1). Teachers provide useful information about academic performance, classroom behaviour, peer relationships and the child's response to authority figures. They may either be interviewed directly, asked to supply a report, or complete a standardized questionnaire such as that of Rutter *et al.* (1970).

Information should also be obtained from any other professionals who have been involved with the child and other family members. Family practitioners may have known the family for years, and can provide relevant details of the family's medical and social history. Members of the extended family, especially grandparents, are often an invaluable source of information, both in terms of what they might have to say, and how they fit into the problem. Meeting grandparents may sometimes be like finding the last piece of a jigsaw.

There was no obvious physical or psychological explanation for Jason's excessive irritability. His asthma, which had started 5 years previously, when aged 3, was reasonably well controlled with daily sodium chromoglycate (an anti-allergy preparation) and occasional inhalations of a bronchodilator. He was able to participate normally in most activities, except during the infrequent occasions when he suffered exacerbations of asthma. There was no obvious family dysfunction or individual psychopathology, but approximately two to three times a month he would suffer bouts of extreme irritability, usually starting on a Sunday evening or Monday morning, during which he was very restless, refused to participate in family activities, complained that no one cared about him, and was unable to sleep. These episodes lasted for about one or two days.

It was pure serendipity that his mother was ill on the day of a review appointment. His grandmother accompanied him and explained how Jason and his younger sister often came to stay for the weekend. Her husband had suffered from asthma for many years and she knew how effective the bronchodilators were in relieving bronchospasm. She loved her daughter very much but was perturbed by her tendency to restrict Jason's use of his medication. To compensate for this, she encouraged him to use his bronchodilator four to five times a day whilst staying with her. It then became clear that his irritability always occurred after staying with his grandmother, and was due to an excessive dosage of medication having an excitatory effect and producing the mood disturbance.

5.3 MULTI-AXIAL DIAGNOSIS

The diagnostic precision of traditional medicine is not so readily available when considering the complex problems of childhood. Indeed, one might argue that this *should* be the case. In earlier times physicians expected to find a single disease entity to account for the patient's signs and symptoms. This disease would be deemed to be caused by disturbance at the molecular, cellular, tissue or organ level. Even now physicians are relieved when everything falls neatly into place under one diagnostic label with one cause. The more comprehensive biopsychosocial model proposed by Engel (1968) (see Chapter 1) has led to the development of a multi-axial diagnostic approach. Indeed, since 1969 at least 16 specific multi-axial systems have been devised for use in diagnosing psychiatric patients (Mezzich, 1988).

The multi-axial diagnostic approach consists of the systematic formulation of the patient's condition in terms of a set of highly informative aspects or variables. Those most commonly used in childhood are the DSM-IIIR (American Psychiatric Association, 1987) and the World Health Organization's ICD-9 (Rutter *et al.*, 1975). These two schemes use similar groupings but have some major differences.

ICD-9 has five axes: (1) clinical psychiatric syndrome; (2) specific delays in development; (3) intellectual level; (4) medical conditions; and (5) abnormal psychosocial situations. DSM-III has the same first two axes but includes mental retardation in axis (1) and personality disorder and types in axis (2). Physical disorders and conditions constitute axis (3). Axes (4) and (5) are available for use in special clinical research settings and provide additional information that may be useful for planning treatment and predicting outcome, i.e.: (4) severity of psychosocial stressors (on seven levels from 'none' to 'catastrophic'); (5) highest level of adaptive functioning in the past year (on seven levels from 'superior' to 'grossly impaired').

DSM-III has now been revised (American Psychiatric Association, 1987) and has added information on intellectual level and illness severity. ICD-10 is due to appear soon (Mezzich, 1988). It is not immediately obvious which approach is to be preferred, for each scheme has advantages and disadvantages (Rutter and Gould, 1985). What matters is that a multidimensional formulation of the problem is prepared, and the use of either multi-axial diagnostic scheme assists this. An example using ICD-9 follows.

Derek, aged 11, has suffered from frequent asthma attacks for seven years. In the previous three months following school transfer he has developed a fear of attending school, and has refused to attend several days a week. He is of normal intelligence but has difficulty with reading, his reading age being 30 months behind his chronological age. Derek's parents are unable to agree on how to manage his school refusal, and argue over many other matters, including his father's long working hours and his mother's over-protectiveness.

A formulation would state that Derek is suffering from separation anxiety and school refusal after a recent change of school. Other aggravating factors include specific reading retardation, with consequent teasing and poor self-image, and anxiety and stress arising from parental conflict. The parents argue about father's lack of involvement in the family and mother's anxiety and over-protectiveness.

The ICD-9 multi-axial diagnosis would read:

(1) school refusal
(2) specific reading retardation
(3) normal intelligence
(4) asthma
(5) discordant intrafamilial relationships
    familial over-involvement
    school stresses

The vital clinical importance of such an approach to diagnosis is that it encourages consideration of *all* factors relevant to the clinical situation, and thus informs clinical decision-making.

The following case example illustrates the use of DSM-III. Sheila, aged 9, had been thoroughly investigated for leg pains and generalized weakness and lethargy, lasting for several months and preventing her from walking. No organic cause could be found, although she had fallen from her pony and bruised her legs. Immediately preceding the onset of symptoms her family were involved in a prolonged and acrimonious legal battle over a grandfather's will, and had for several months been trying to sell their house. Her parents were preoccupied with the problem and had little time for Sheila; her two elder sisters were irritated by her continuous complaints of pain and general misery.

The formulation would read: Sheila is suffering from psychogenic pain following a fall from her pony. There are no medical abnormalities and her level of development is normal, but she does have a somewhat passive approach to life, with only one or two friends. Her family is preoccupied with a legal battle and the sale of their house, and spend very little time listening to or discussing each other's anxieties. The pains appear to be Sheila's way of expressing her distress and gaining parental attention.

The DSM-III diagnosis is:

(1) psychogenic pain disorder
(2) passive personality
(3) no abnormality
(4) psychosocial stressors; intrafamilial conflict; inadequate intrafamilial communication; moderate
(5) functioned quite well at school and home prior to symptoms; fair

Different professionals will have different priorities, and may tend to reorder the axes to suit their speciality. Thus a physician is likely to use a scheme that places the medical diagnoses on the first axis. The order of the scheme matters less than that all aspects are included.

5.4 SUMMARY

Whilst in traditional medicine diagnosis is usually obtained by a combination of history taking, physical examination and specific investigations, in childhood disorders a more complex and comprehensive approach is required. Attention must be paid not only to the development of the problem but also to its context. The role of the family and others in maintaining, aggravating or alleviating the problem must be assessed if the full picture is to be uncovered. Diagnosis is made using a multi-axial scheme and is best presented as a formulation.

In the next chapter we describe how to use an integrated approach to treatment.

CHAPTER 6

A Psychosomatic Approach to Treatment

Inferior doctors treat the disease of a patient
Mediocre doctors treat the patient as a person
Superior doctors treat the community as a whole
(Huang Dee (2600 BC) Nai Chung—*1st Chinese Medical Text)*

GUIDE FOR THE READER

In this chapter we acknowledge ancient Eastern wisdom, emphasize the need for a psychosomatic treatment approach, summarize the roles of the different mental health professionals, and discuss how to help parents who are resistant to such an approach, without engaging in unproductive argument.

6.1 INTRODUCTION

A psychosomatic approach to treatment involves paying attention from the start to physical, developmental, social and psychological factors, just as does the psychosomatic approach to assessment described in Chapter 5. Once the assessment is complete the formulation, or multi-axial diagnosis, should be shared with the parents and, if appropriate, with the child concerned. Because of the frequent complexity and non-specificity of presenting problems, it is easy to avoid offering a diagnosis or formulation. Indeed, not infrequently further interviews or sessions are recommended without any multi-axial diagnosis or formulation being made, or any rationale for therapy offered. Successful outcome is more likely if time, patience and understanding are freely available.

6.2 CONVEYING THE DIAGNOSIS

A clear and comprehensive explanation should be provided, covering all aspects of the problem. The following example concerns a 10-year-old girl with recurrent abdominal pain:

> We have fully investigated Jenny's stomach aches and fortunately we found no physical cause. This is good news because we have excluded serious disease. Stomach aches at this age with no physical cause are quite common. Indeed 1 in 10 of all children aged 10 have this problem. Sometimes it is called 'abdominal migraine' or 'spastic colon' or 'periodic syndrome'. There are many different names. It seems that the muscles inside the abdomen go into spasm or a cramp when the person is under stress or is upset. It seems to run in families, and we frequently find that one or other parent had a similar problem as a child, or has headaches or migraines as an adult. It is usually brought on by worries or upsets. In Jenny's case it is clear that there have been some recent worries; her grandfather's illness has been upsetting for you all, and she is quite worried about changing schools in a few months time. As you say she finds it quite hard to talk about worries and they have become locked up inside her, giving her these stomach aches.

This explanation includes a description of the problem, and reference to the developmental, hereditary, physical and psychosocial factors. It avoids the dichotomy of 'either physical or psychological'. It can be elaborated if necessary, but it is wise to start with a relatively concise explanation. It is difficult for anxious parents to listen to, understand and remember long speeches; far better to encourage questions and a dialogue than to deliver a lecture.

Many parents have no difficulty accepting the need for a comprehensive approach to their child's problem or for psychological treatments. Several will be seeking psychological help. Some, however, are at least ambivalent to the idea, whilst others are completely rejecting. Without full parental acceptance of such a need, the chances of the child improving are considerably impaired. Indeed, such parents may prefer to seek a second, third or even fourth opinion. This attitude not only delays the introduction of effective treatment but also reinforces the problem by both the continuous attention to symptoms, and the stresses imposed by further unpleasant, painful or even hazardous investigations.

6.3 CONVINCING THE DOUBTING PARENT

Convincing doubting parents of the need for psychological help is an important but difficult task. Figure 6.1 outlines the sequences involved. There is no problem when parents accept the need, and therapy can be initiated straight away. A different pathway is necessary for those parents who are uncertain or who reject the idea.

Having given as clear as possible an explanation, it is usually obvious whether or not the parents are able to accept it. The non-accepting parents will either immediately launch into a series of questions which explicitly doubt the

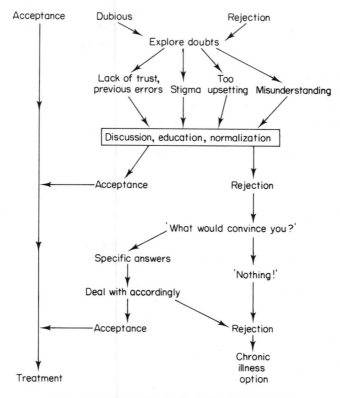

Figure 6.1 Convincing the doubting parent

diagnosis, or frankly criticize it. Non-verbal communications are often equally revealing. 'Dubious' or 'rejecting' parents may stay quiet at this stage, but facial expressions usually make obvious their reactions. It is important to acknowledge and explore the parents' doubts. The most common reasons for non-acceptance include misunderstanding what has been said, a lack of trust in doctors, often linked to previous errors, and the stigma and distress attached to a psychological explanation.

Misunderstandings need to be recognized early, and the most useful way of doing this after offering the initial formulation is to ask the parents whether they have any questions or want any clarification; invariably they do. The tone and content of the questions or comments not only reveal their attitude to the formulation but may also give clues to possible misunderstandings. For example, on hearing the explanation that Jenny's stomach-aches are due to stress, a parent may respond by saying 'So you think she's imagining it?' Common variations include 'You reckon there's nothing wrong then?' or 'Is she malingering?', 'So you're saying its all in the mind', 'You mean she's making it up?', or even 'Are you telling us she's crazy?' (or an equivalent euphemism).

Lack of trust is often due to previous errors. A close relative may have suffered or even died from an undiagnosed or incorrectly diagnosed condition. There may have been similar or even identical symptoms. A parent may say 'you think it's just nerves, but they said that about my mother before they found that her stomach was riddled with cancer'.

The *stigma* associated with 'mental illness' dies hard. For some it is a source of shame, best denied or avoided, and for others it is simply too devastating to accept. Stigma is often compounded by parental misunderstanding (see above).

Distress—some parents find such a diagnosis so upsetting they cannot respond in any but a negative manner. They will often perceive the implication that they are to blame—'You're saying that it is our fault then?' Even when they do not blame themselves, they may still be overwhelmed by feelings resulting from misunderstanding or stigma.

At this stage the interviewer should have some idea of the causes of the parents' negative response, and should aim to help overcome them. This is best done by a process of discussion, clarification, normalization and education. A didactic lecture or statement is never as convincing or as effective as discussing the relevant issues. Clarification involves distinguishing between, on the one hand, stress and distress and their effects, and on the other psychiatric illness. This is linked to normalization. One can make such statements as 'Everyone experiences stress reactions from time to time—when I've had a bad day I get a headache. I wonder what you get'. A simple explanation of the psychophysiological processes (see Chapter 2) may also help.

By now some parents will be able to accept the need for a psychological input, whilst others will remain dubious or determinedly rejecting. A helpful question at this stage is 'What would convince you?' A few parents will give specific answers such as 'A brain scan' or 'A biopsy'. Others might say 'I don't know' or 'Nothing'. If specific tests are mentioned it is worth doing these providing that they are not dangerous, unpleasant, or in any other way contraindicated. Those who do not know what would convince them should be encouraged to discuss it further together until they can either specify or realize that nothing would provide such assurance.

Once parents move to an accepting position, treatment can start. A small group, however, reject the concept whatever efforts are made to convince them that the condition is psychological in nature. Under these circumstances further discussion, explanation or entreaty is unlikely to help. If no other physician has seen the child it is certainly advisable to recommend seeking a second opinion, but otherwise further opinion-seeking should not be encouraged. It can, however, be predicted. It is sometimes useful to say:

> I do understand that you find it hard to accept my view and that of others who have seen Jenny before; I'm sure that you'll continue to seek further opinions in the

hope that you'll find one that is easier to accept. However, that won't be in her interests, for it means she will have repeats of the investigations, some of which as you know are quite unpleasant or have risks attached to them; even more importantly she will not be getting the treatment that she needs. It is likely that she will therefore remain unwell. Eventually you may then have to accept that she could stay this way for a very long time, and you would be wise to plan accordingly. If, however, you do change your mind I would be happy to arrange the appropriate treatment. In the meantime if you would like some help in adjusting to her new situation of long-term ill health, that also can be provided.

The prediction of further 'doctor-shopping' and chronic ill health occasionally helps parents to realize the counter-productiveness of their approach. Alternatively, they may be able to accept the relatively non-threatening offer of long-term support, which can gradually turn into an exploration of psychological issues.

An additional technique involves predicting the possibility of the emergence at a later date of a specific and physically treatable disorder, whilst indicating that in the meantime the family's task is to help the child cope with the present situation. In the following example one of the authors uses an experience he had in his own family.

Standing at a blackboard drawing (Figure 6.2) A.F. says:

Let me introduce you to a concept that may be new to you. My daughter, when she was 23, went for a check-up, because she felt weak, had no energy and found getting through the day a struggle. The doctor discovered anaemia but couldn't find a reason for it. She was given iron by mouth but her anaemia did not respond and she did not feel any better. For two years her condition could not be diagnosed, in spite of numerous blood tests and other investigations. She was not living at home at the time and we worried about her a great deal. Bless her heart, she continued to work and maintained her normal activities, but we could see that she was really suffering.

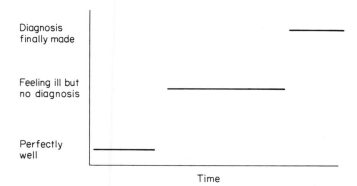

Figure 6.2 Awaiting the diagnosis

Then one day she told me that her hands had been stiff and sore in the mornings for the past week. When I looked at them, I knew immediately that she had rheumatoid arthritis, and that it was the cause of her anaemia, even though it had not shown us what it was for two years. Children may stay in the never-never land of undiagnosable illness whilst continuing symptoms for many years before the true nature of the illness shows itself.

In many cases the symptoms just go away without a firm diagnosis being made. Waiting for the disease to show itself is an approach that is safe and would cause your daughter the least pain and possible injury. [If you are following this case as psychologist or social worker, a point to be emphasized is that the physician will continue to be involved and is therefore always available to check the patient when you or the parents are concerned about a physical complaint.]

In the meantime we must decide what are the best ways for her to spend her days. You know that the longer you stay away from things the harder it is to pick them up again. If my daughter had not kept going she would have been out of the normal flow of things for two and a half years, because it was six months after the diagnosis was made before she started feeling well. Your options for your daughter range from letting her stay home and worrying about her symptoms all day, to carrying on normal daily activities for her age. My daughter chose to stay on and is now credit manager for a local business, with a good salary. I don't believe that she would be there now if she had given in to her symptoms. What do you think that we should do?

The parents are obviously being steered towards returning their child to school and a normal daily routine.

Usually such work is and can be done by one person but in an ideal world it is best done jointly by a paediatrician or physician and a mental health professional (Bingley *et al.*, 1980; Dungar *et al.*, 1986). This method has the advantage of demonstrating to sceptical parents how psychological and somatic factors may be linked, not only in theory but also in practice. It shows how seriously professionals take the interaction between the two, and it prevents the parents splitting the professionals by reporting to one professional that the other had told them something quite different. It is also helpful for the mental health professional to observe the parental response to the paediatrician's explanation without immediately becoming involved in the discussion. In this way it is possible to start understanding any parental resistance.

The paediatrician gives the initial explanation and formulation, encouraging any questions. Gradually the mental health professional can become involved, initially perhaps by promoting discussion between the parents and paediatrician, and then making empathic observations, such as: 'I can see that you are very worried about Jenny and that you want to be absolutely sure that we have the correct diagnosis. Is there anything that you would like to ask before we go any further?' The psychiatrist or equivalent who jumps in at the deep end or is thrown in by the paediatrician is likely to have to swim to the side very quickly. For example; Dr Fosson: 'This is my colleague Dr Lask, the psychiatrist. He wants to ask you some questions.' Dr Lask: 'Hello. Has anyone in the family had nervous problems?'

The process of helping parents move from their medical view of the problem to a wider perspective requires patience, subtlety, skill and empathy.

6.4 WHO DOES WHAT?

Mental health professionals include psychiatrists, psychologists, social workers, psychotherapists and psychiatric nurses. Whilst their skills and training vary considerably there is often substantial overlap. For example, each should be able to carry out the assessment procedure described in Chapter 5, and each should have a degree of expertise in one or more of the treatment techniques described in Chapters 7–10.

A psychiatrist should be competent in both physical and psychological assessment of the child, and familiar with medications described in Chapter 10 and one or more of the other treatment approaches. Psychologists are trained in the use of instruments for intelligence testing and other aspects of intellectual functioning, and will usually have an expertise in behavioural techniques (Chapter 7) or individual psychotherapy (Chapter 9). They are usually familiar with the educational system and available resources. Social workers will be familiar with legislation pertaining to children and will usually have skills in parent counselling (Chapter 7) and family therapy (Chapter 8). Psychotherapists have a specific training in the practical application of psychoanalytic theory (e.g., Freud, 1966; Klein, 1948). Psychiatric nurses will differ in what they have to offer, depending upon whether they are based in a hospital, clinic or community setting. They should all be able to offer one or more treatments, whilst those in the community will be familiar with community-based resources.

To whom the child or family is referred depends to some extent on availability, so that, for example, if a paediatrician and psychologist work very closely, the paediatrician is very likely to refer to the psychologist. However, the psychologist should make a thorough assessment before deciding on a particular treatment. Sadly, it is all too frequent for mental health professionals to offer only that treatment in which they have an interest or expertise, rather than referring on to a colleague. There are specific indications (and sometimes contraindications) for each treatment modality, and these are discussed in the relevant chapters. In many instances a combination of treatments may be necessary. For example, in nearly all cases some parental counselling is mandatory. This may be offered in the context of family therapy, but otherwise should occur in its own right, regardless of what other therapy is offered. When children are being treated in individual therapy or with medication, the parents should always be seen on a regular basis to discuss management and progress. Liaison with the school, or advice about change of school, or remedial teaching, is often required as an adjunct to treatment.

6.5 LIAISON

To ensure the success of an integrated approach to treatment, there must be effective liaison between professional colleagues. Successful liaison is dependent upon mutual respect and understanding, open, direct and frequent communication, and clear planning with mutually agreed aims and regular reviews. Inappropriate expectations of what colleagues have to offer, or lack of understanding of and respect for their skills and training, may all lead to subsequent disappointments and frustration. Hierarchies between professional staff can aggravate such problems.

Given the differences in emphasis between the two disciplines it is hardly surprising that difficulties arise. Comparing stereotypes of medical practice with those of mental health practice, a polarization of emphasis becomes evident: body versus mind; organ or system versus the whole child; individual versus family; immediate versus long-term; life or death versus quality of life; active treatment versus passive involvement; cure versus care. In addition mental health practice has its own jargon, a different conceptual framework, lack of diagnostic precision, lack of evaluation of therapy, and a reactive preoccupation with epidemiology and statistics. Clinical practice too often takes place behind closed doors, and may last for an inordinate length of time.

A typical scenario might involve a paediatrician referring a child with recurrent abdominal pain to the mental health service, hoping that an early assessment will lead to rapid resolution. The paediatrician may not know of the child's deprived background or stress-laden environment, whilst the mental health professional may have failed to convey to the paediatrician the complexities involved in assessing and attempting to resolve such problems.

Mutual respect and understanding is best achieved by regular meetings which allow for direct and open communication between colleagues. At the very least there should be frequent correspondence about shared cases. This should include statements about diagnosis or formulation, outlines of aims, advice about treatment and reviews of progress. It is vital for the mental health consultant to avoid jargon, and to provide clear reports, with practical advice for liaison and management given in language that is easily understood by the referrer.

A report that states that 'this child's denial of his inner reality, with repressed libidinal instincts and unresolved oedipal fantasies, inevitably impairs his reality adaptation, with subsequent dissociation, and loss of use of his limbs' is of no value whatsoever to anyone but its author (and even that is questionable). At the other extreme is the diagnostically precise but equally unhelpful 'this child is suffering from a mixed conduct and emotional disorder'.

In hospital or clinical settings the ideal forum for liaison is a frequent, regular meeting of multidisciplinary staff (Bingley *et al.*, 1980; Dungar *et al.*, 1986). Where different agencies or practices share cases, every effort should be made to organize meetings either on a regular or ad hoc basis. A successful outcome for a shared case is far more likely if professionals meet to discuss the management. Without such meetings it is all too easy for conflict and confusion to occur. Liaison may also be enhanced by mental health professionals attending ward rounds or clinics, to learn more about 'how the other half lives', to become familiar with themes and problems, and to offer a service.

6.6 WHEN AND HOW TO REFER

Whilst most paediatricians or physicians wish to apply an integrated approach to treatment, many would consider themselves unable to use psychological treatment as part of their everyday practice, through lack of time, skill or knowledge. Certainly any doctor who sees children regularly should become familiar with very basic approaches, such as counselling parents, utilizing simple behaviour-modification techniques (Chapter 7) and helping children to discuss their problems (Chapter 9) (see also an excellent paper by Wolff, 1986). Nonetheless the important question remains as to when referrals should be made to mental health professionals.

For all but the most psychologically skilled paediatricians and physicians we consider the following to be indications for referral:

(1) Severe emotional disturbance—it is essential in such circumstances to seek the opinion of a child psychiatrist, who can carry out a formal assessment and advise on appropriate treatment (Chapters 7–10).
(2) Obvious family dysfunction—where it is clear that family members are in distress or the dysfunction is causing or aggravating ill health, referral to a family therapist of whatever professional background is indicated.
(3) Suspected or proven learning difficulties, or educational problems or developmental delay—in all such cases a psychologist's opinion and help should be sought (Chapter 5).
(4) Undiagnosed illness—when physical examination and investigation prove unhelpful, it is wise to seek the opinion of a psychiatrist, psychologist or social worker, in an attempt to understand better the possible contribution of psychosocial factors, and to provide relevant treatment.
(5) Poorly controlled illness—when a diagnosed illness has been appropriately treated, and yet remains poorly controlled, it is probable that psychosocial factors are making a significant contribution, either in terms of stress and distress or non-compliance; again the opinion and help of a psychiatrist, psychologist or social worker is indicated.
(6) Illness in which psychosocial factors are obviously relevant—it should go without saying that this is a prime indication for referral to the appropriate mental health professional.

(7) On diagnosis of a long-term or fatal illness—the implications of serious illness are overwhelming for children and their families (Chapter 4); it is almost certain that there will be major psychosocial sequelae, which are not only troublesome and distressing but also may aggravate or intensify the illness.

The mechanisms of referral depend on individual circumstances. The ideal is in the context of regular liaison meetings (Bingley *et al.*, 1980; Dungar *et al.*, 1986). If these are not possible every effort should still be made to discuss the referral, giving as much information as possible, and for the first consultation to be attended jointly by the referrer and the mental health professional (see section 6.3). If this is not possible it is essential that the referrer explains clearly to the parents the reason for this action, and helps them to express and explore any doubts.

In turn the professional to whom the child is referred should make every effort to help the child and family feel at ease, and give them sufficient opportunity to state their views. However, it is unhelpful to become involved in arguments about whether or not the referral is indicated. This will only reinforce defensiveness and resistance, and certainly does not help to instil trust or confidence in the mental health professional. Far better in such circumstances to ask the referrer to see the parents again, preferably in a joint interview (section 6.3).

In conclusion, referrals should be made in any of the situations described above, and as early as possible in the process. If in doubt about whether or not to refer, it is wise to err on the side of making the referral, for little is lost by doing so; delay, however, only prolongs the problem and reduces the chances of successful outcome.

6.7 CASE ILLUSTRATION

Many of the points made in this chapter are illustrated in the following case example.

Tracy, aged 11, had a seven-year history of severe eczema with frequent exacerbations and only short periods of remission. Full investigation revealed some specific allergens, but careful allergen avoidance measures had little effect. The family doctor referred Tracy for a second opinion, and the dermatologist changed the medication, with no effect. Eventually the parents independently sought the opinion of a paediatric dermatologist. She concluded that psychosocial factors were exacerbating the problem and proposed obtaining a psychiatric opinion. The parents were resistant to this suggestion, but shortly afterwards Tracy suffered a severe exacerbation, with the need for further hospitalization. The paediatrician explained that an essential part of the re-assessment and treatment would be full psychosocial assessment.

The psychiatrist carried out an individual assessment of Tracy, and then a full family assessment. Because the school report indicated classroom difficulties, a psychological assessment was also arranged. Once the assessments were complete, the following formulation was made:

> Tracy's severe eczema clearly has allergic origins but appears to be exacerbated by the following stresses: (1) she is teased at school and has few friends; (2) there is evidence of specific learning difficulties, in that she has trouble with both reading and spelling, although her intelligence is well within the normal range; (3) she is very distressed by her illness, and feels hopeless about the future; (4) her parents are unable to help her express her distress, which remains suppressed but intense; (5) her mother feels guilty that she seems unable to protect Tracy from exposure to allergens; (6) her father is irritated by his wife's over-involvement with Tracy, believing that Tracy should be encouraged to get on with it, rather than allowing herself to be handicapped; (7) her older brother tries to stop her from scratching herself, leading to arguments between them, and more determined scratching with consequent worsening of the eczema.
>
> The following management is recommended:
>
> (1) Liaise with Tracy's school, recommend remedial help for her learning difficulties, and discuss with her teachers how to handle peer group teasing;
> (2) Offer relaxation or hypnotherapy (Chapter 9) for relief of itching, and an opportunity for Tracy to find ways of expressing outwardly her feelings rather than holding them in.
> (3) Social skills training (Chapter 9) to help Tracy know how to respond to teasing.
> (4) Family therapy (Chapter 8) to help the family to identify and share distress, and to help parents adopt a mutually agreed and consistent approach to managing Tracy's response to her illness, and the sibling arguments (Chapter 7).
> (5) Continue with medical management of eczema, although it is anticipated that this could be reduced once the treatments have taken effect.

This treatment package integrated a number of different therapeutic techniques, details of which are described fully in succeeding chapters. Its success was dependent on successful liaison between professional colleagues (see section 6.5) as much as their individual skills. Implementation of appropriate treatment had been delayed by the initial failure to refer to a mental health professional, and then by the parents' resistance to the idea. Nonetheless they were impressed by the thoroughness of the assessment and the comprehensiveness of the treatment offered, and they cooperated fully.

Tracy's eczema improved considerably as changes occurred in other areas. Her family became more responsive to her emotional needs, the school arranged for remedial help, and she gained confidence in herself as she learned self-relaxation and hypnosis to control the itching, and techniques for handling the teasing. At one year follow-up she had required no further hospitalization, and was on a reduced dose of medication.

6.8 SUMMARY

Treatment should always be considered from a comprehensive perspective, with attention being paid to physical, developmental, social and psychological factors. The process of convincing parents of the need for such an approach is sometimes difficult and requires patience, subtlety, empathy and skill. Psychological treatments should be determined by the needs of the child and family rather than the therapist's orientation. The parents should always be involved.

The final four chapters of this book deal with the main treatments available for children and their families.

CHAPTER 7

Helping Parents

Children begin by loving their parents. After a time they judge them.
Rarely, if ever, do they forgive them (Oscar Wilde)

GUIDE FOR THE READER

Wilde's elegant cynicism indicates the daunting task awaiting parents. When illness complicates their task yet further, a sine qua non of the treatment process is their involvement. In this chapter we describe the basic principles of parenting, and describe some common and useful techniques for parents to use when faced with their children's physical problems. Marital therapy, which focuses on the couple's own relationship, rather than how they work together as parents, is discussed in Chapter 8.

7.1 INTRODUCTION

Given the central role of the parents in a child's life, it is clearly appropriate to work closely with them on children's problems. Whether this is done in the context of parent counselling or family therapy depends on the circumstances. There is no justification for excluding parents from the treatment process, even when the child is in intensive individual therapy (Chapter 9). Specific indications for family therapy are discussed in Chapter 8, and in all other instances parents should be seen on a regular basis. Examples include when a child is receiving a special form of individual help, such as individual psychotherapy, or behaviour modification, or when the child has a specific problem such as a developmental delay, or a chronic or recurrent illness.

Before effective parental counselling can commence, therapists need to be aware of certain basic and vital principles of parenting, and to join with the parents to engage them in the necessary work. It is helpful to have some information about parental background and how this influences their current attitudes and behaviour, as well as information about the problem and how it is handled. This helps determine which technique is likely to be most useful—

91

straightforward advice, behaviour modification techniques or parental counselling.

Most of what is said in this chapter applies to both one- and two-parent
families. Certainly the task is far harder for single parents, and acknowledgement of and allowance for this must always be made. In addition, particular problems can arise when parents are separated, or step-parents or other
partners become part of the family. Under these circumstances it is essential
that the adults negotiate as to who is in charge, who has parental rights, and the
extent of those rights. These decisions should also be explained to the children.

7.2 BASIC PRINCIPLES OF PARENTING

Although child-rearing is probably the single most important and difficult task
that most people tackle, they do so with virtually no preparation or training save
experiences buried deep in childhood. Good parents seem to rely on basic
principles as well as behavioural patterns learned during childhood training.
The most important of these are cooperation, communication and consistency.

The parents need to work together as a team, supporting and helping each
other, neither allowing the children to split them, nor trying to get the children
to take sides. They need to share problems and decisions, identify and resolve
conflicts, and remain consistent both in their manner of handling situations at
any one moment and over time. Problems may arise or be aggravated when
parents are unsupportive or inconsistent, and when they allow or encourage
children to take sides, or fail to identify and resolve problems or conflicts.

James, aged 12, had frequent headaches, particularly on school mornings.
His mother tended to cosset him, allowing him to stay in bed and miss school,
whilst his father preferred to ignore the headaches and insist James go to school
as normal. The parents would then criticize each other's approach, and end up
arguing. James' headaches intensified.

Open and direct communication between the parents, and between parent
and child, is another facet of successful parenting. Sharing of feelings, both
positive and negative, is far healthier than 'bottling up'.

Joe, aged 6, presented with 'drop attacks'; he would turn pale, complain of
feeling dizzy and then fall to the floor. His mother, who had experienced
considerable trauma at the hands of her own parents, was terrified of her own
anger. Whenever anything happened that irritated her, she would go silent and
withdraw from the situation. Her husband described her face as 'like a mask of
fury'. Joe's episodes occurred most commonly at these times when his mother
was feeling angry. Clearly Joe found his mother's reaction puzzling and frightening. Although the reason for his initial drop attack was not known, it is likely
that the problem was being maintained by his mother's abnormal reaction to
anger.

In many instances paying attention to these basic principles may be enough to overcome the problem, but correctly joining with the parents is an essential prerequisite to any successful intervention.

7.3 THE THERAPEUTIC ALLIANCE

The rapport-building phase is extensive and follows the general recommendations outlined in Chapter 5. Important aspects of developing a working alliance with parents centre on understanding the parents' attitudes and emotions (a respectful and gentle handling of the parents' feelings and position is doubly important because this models how they should relate to their child). When accompanying a sick child to a consultation, parents may feel the illness or problem represents their failure as parents. Accompanying feelings may include anxiety, sadness, hostility, protectiveness and helplessness. The therapeutic alliance is encouraged by the therapist (1) recognizing the dominant feeling currently held, (2) assuming they are doing their best, and (3) presuming that their intentions are good. These professional attitudes and sensitivity to the parents' feelings form the underpinning of strategies for building rapport.

The following example illustrates the setting up of a relationship with parents. The family consists of somewhat hostile parents and a 12-year-old boy with poor school attendance of eight months duration. During the period in question, the boy's complaints had shifted from sore throat to abdominal pain and diarrhoea, and finally to being picked on by peers at school. This case may be approached as follows. After the chief complaint and some of the present problem has been described, a facilitating statement might be, 'You are obviously concerned for Bobby, and you have always tried to take good care of him. Since he has been ill you have taken him to several different doctors and followed their advice trying to get Bobby well. Having him still ill must be disappointing to you . . . I should think you might be a bit put out that none of those doctors have been able to help you get Bobby better. It must seem like medicine has failed you!' After some indication of agreement, the interviewer can proceed. When consensus on a therapeutic goal is reached, the remainder of the contract is secured by the therapist (1) stating that the parents are in charge, (2) offering explanations and suggestions for ways of proceeding, and (3) advising of the need for joint decisions.

Many parents are only too eager to describe their own experiences as children and they should not be discouraged from so doing. Frequently the key to the problem is revealed as the story is told. Much information can be obtained by asking such questions as 'Were you happy as a child?', 'Who was the boss in your family?', 'Who looked after you when you were upset?'

An example of a parent revealing the key to current problems while describing her own childhood is that of Evelyn, aged 12, with a three-year history of anorexia nervosa. She had a brother, aged 15, and parents with long-standing marital problems. Her mother had remained deeply attached and very close to her own mother, who herself had an unhappy relationship with her husband, Evelyn's grandfather. Evelyn complained that her mother never gave her any freedom or sense of being separate: 'My mother knows me better than I do.' This three-generational pattern of over-involvement and not letting go was obviously relevant in that Evelyn's mother had no experience of being separate from her own mother, and therefore could not help Evelyn to be so. Evelyn's response was to develop an illness in which she had some control and autonomy, at least over her own body.

Once satisfactory rapport had been achieved and sufficient information is available, it is possible to choose the most suitable counselling technique. Often straightforward advice is sufficient, sometimes a behavioural programme is indicated, and occasionally more formal parental counselling is necessary. Each of these is discussed in turn. Every effort should be made to involve both parents in the process.

7.4 ADVISING PARENTS

This is probably the most common technique used in face-to-face work with parents. Often parents need simple and clear advice from an expert on how to handle a situation. For example, the parents of James, cited above, whose headaches occurred on school mornings only needed to be told 'You must work together; you can't expect him to get better as long as one of you takes one line, and the other the opposite.' They were able to agree on a policy of working together, with father, who was better at firmness, giving him a cuddle and then saying 'Now you must get up', whilst mother, who was better at sympathy, acknowledging James' distress but supporting father in taking a firm line. In this manner they worked together, distributing their resources in the most compatible way.

The type of advice varies with the circumstances, and clinicians must use their judgement as to what is appropriate.

An example of correcting parental inconsistency is the case of a 7-year-old with enuresis. No physical reason could be found for Simon wetting his bed three to four nights a week, and everyone agreed that he had now become very anxious about it. His parents could not decide on whether to ignore the bed-wetting on the basis that drawing attention to it might exacerbate his anxiety, or to reward him on the mornings he was dry, thus taking a positive approach. They fluctuated between the two and in consequence handled the situation inconsistently. Both views were reasonable, but only one technique should have been used. The therapist advised that it mattered less which approach they adopted, and more that they agreed on which they should use, and that they should apply one or other approach consistently. They chose to reward dry nights, and after a few weeks the enuresis stopped.

An example of improving communications through advice is that of Janice, 13, who consistently refused to have physiotherapy for her cystic fibrosis. Her parents, who were rightly determined that she should have the treatment, found themselves in regular battles with her. It transpired that in their eagerness to implement the therapy they had not attempted to find out why Janice was so resistant, having assumed that it was predominantly the discomfort. The therapist advised the parents to spend some time calmly discussing with her what she found so upsetting about it. It transpired that during one hospitalization another child had suffered from a 'ruptured lung', and Janice was convinced that the daily 'thumping' would do the same to her. Once this concern had been expressed it was possible for her parents, with the advice of the physician and physiotherapist, to explain that the other child had a different problem and that this would not happen to her. This was sufficient to help Janice accept the therapy.

A topic of particular importance for susceptible or ill children is the strong emphasis on explicit discussions of feelings. These can provide an 'immunization' against somatization, ease depressive symptoms in chronically ill children, or replace physical complaints as a means of obtaining nurturance. In practice, empathic communications involve: (1) parents estimating the child's emotional state from facial expression, posture, etc., or trying to imagine how they would feel in the child's position; and (2) expressing these feelings to the child in a way that fosters openness and validates the child's reactions. For example, if the child comes in from play upset, the parent might say 'Something seems to be upsetting you' and the child responds with 'They made fun of me because I couldn't hit the ball'; the parent might continue with 'Poor you; that must have been embarrassing.' If the child's experience contained positive aspects, the parent could praise the child by saying 'I'm proud of you', or could encourage the child to depend more on their own standards and judgement by saying 'You must feel proud of yourself.' The latter is important because it tends to decrease the child's dependence on external confirmation. Children develop self-respect as a consequence of their parents valuing their skills and strengths, showing them respect as individuals with rights and privileges, as well as needs and responsibilities.

Direct advice to parents can be enhanced by input from other sources such as programmes of instruction for parents (Dindmeyer and Mckay, 1982) and self-help books for parents (e.g., Gould, 1982; Lask, 1985).

7.5 BEHAVIOUR APPROACHES

We have chosen to include behaviour approaches in this chapter because in our opinion parents should always be involved in their application. The definitions and principles are the same, however, whoever supervises the treatment. The techniques of behaviour modification are based on the practical application of learning theory (Bandura, 1974) in which the basic assumption is that behaviour is learned in a mechanistic way. Complex behaviours are understood as a chain reaction of stimuli and responses. There is no attempt to find hidden meanings or tackle underlying problems. The basic aims are to stop undesirable behaviour and encourage desirable behaviour. Assessment consists of analysing such chain reactions, whilst therapy utilizes basic concepts such as desensitization, modelling, flooding, reinforcement, shaping and extinction (Yule, 1985).

In the clinical application of these methods it is helpful to assess: (1) the interventions previously tried by the parents; (2) earlier advice received from professional and lay sources; (3) parental therapeutic prejudices; and (4) their familiarity with the selected technique. This may obviate embarrassment and lost time; for example: 'We've tried that already and it didn't work' or 'That's just bribery.'

7.5.1 Desensitization

This involves a gradual approach to a feared object while the child is relaxed, and is based on the impossibility of feeling anxious and relaxed at the same time. If, for example, a child develops abdominal pain whenever he attempts to go to school, a desensitization programme may be initiated. The child is taught self-relaxation, and then exposed, initially in imagination and then in reality, to a programme of gradual school return.

The 'imagination' work is based on helping the child draw up a hierarchy of anxiety-provoking situations, starting with only the mildly worrying and ending with what creates dread. Martin, aged 12, chose waking up on a school morning as the first step, which he rated as 4 out of 10 for worry, putting on his school uniform scored 5, catching the bus to school 7, seeing the school 8, entering the school 9, and being in the classroom 10. Each step is imagined whilst in a relaxed state, until it no longer causes anxiety, when the next step is introduced.

The steps of actual exposure can follow the same sequence, starting with the least frightening. Alternatively the child could simply visit the school at the end of the school day and then come home with a friend. Classes could slowly be added and the adult gradually withdrawn at a pace the child can tolerate. The advantage of either approach is that the child knows that he can withdraw to the 'safe' environment of home immediately after exposure, until he feels that he can cope. The critical components are the *gradual exposure* to the feared situation whilst in a *relaxed* state.

7.5.2 Modelling

This is the exposure of the child to the desired behaviour. For example, the fearful or phobic child is exposed to other children happily playing in the feared situation and is gradually encouraged to join in. A sick child with a needle phobia who needs frequent blood tests is treated by encouraging the child to watch other children, or indeed a parent, having venepunctures. Modelling and desensitization combined seem to be particularly effective for such fears (Graziano *et al.*, 1979).

7.5.3 Flooding

This involves bringing the child into immediate and intensive contact with the feared object. It is not often used in childhood, and there are obvious ethical issues to be considered. However, it is an effective treatment for school phobia, providing that it is sensitively used, with the parents and school staff being firm but understanding, and supportive of each other and the child. Many a child with recurrent abdominal pain or headache, the origins of which lie in school phobia, has managed to return to school, once the parents have understood the rationale of the treatment, prepared themselves for vigorous protestations and developed the resolve to persevere.

Hannah had been school-phobic for four years. All treatments had failed. Eventually the parents were advised to take her to school the next day and, with the agreement of school staff, insist she stay there whatever her protestations. Despite her tears, screaming, threats to run away or kill herself, they persevered. The school kindly but firmly supported her parents. Within four days there were no further problems.

7.5.4 Reinforcement

This involves the immediate provision of desired attention, praise, token or tangible rewards for desired behaviour. For example, a child with cystic fibrosis who resists physiotherapy can be encouraged to accept it by the immediate reinforcement of compliance with praise or a token. When a predetermined number of tokens have been earned, these are exchanged for an appropriate reward (positive reinforcement). Alternatively, a reward can be withdrawn from a child when he produces an unacceptable behaviour. For example, a toddler who ruminates may really enjoy having his back rubbed. This can be done by an adult who is very careful to stop the pleasant back rubbing whenever the child ruminates. The aim is that the child will decrease behaviour which leads to a decrease in pleasure.

Certain performance characteristics of a reinforcement programme are important: (1) if a behaviour does not already exist in the child's repertoire, reinforcement cannot cause it to appear; (2) if the target behaviour does not occur, neither the reward nor part of it should be given; (3) rewards must be individualized to the child—there is no point giving cuddles as a reward if the child does not like cuddling; (4) social rewards (praise, smiles, cuddles) should be coupled with any tangible reward; (5) tangible rewards should be repeatedly rewarding to the child and easily repeated by the parent; (6) details of some aspects of the programme, especially the rewards, require frequent updating to remain effective; (7) intermittent rewards are more effective than consistent reinforcers, after the behaviour is well established.

Most reinforcement programmes are initially successful but often fail later because of parental fatigue or flagging motivation. In some such families it can be helpful also to reward the parents. This can readily be done socially by warmth and praise. Although value-judgements may hinder the use of tangible rewards for parents by many therapists, needy parents are particularly likely to benefit. The therapist's modelling of the behaviour he is requesting of the parents is particularly powerful (O'Dell, 1974).

7.5.5 Shaping

This is a variation of the positive reinforcement technique, in which *approximations* to the desired behaviour are rewarded. Rewards can be given for a child's *partially* successful efforts; or a graded programme of reinforcement is designed to shape a child's behaviour, as this example of a 6-year-old who soils his pants illustrates. The behavioural sequence to be identified is: sensing the need, going to the toilet, undressing, excreting, cleaning and redressing. As an initial step he would be rewarded for zipping up his pants. Subsequent reinforcement would require the successful completing of steps added in a retrograde fashion, but the reward would always be given on completion of the last step.

7.5.6 Extinction

This is the withdrawal of positive reinforcement for undesired behaviour. If, for example, a child hyperventilates whenever he is disciplined, and in consequence the parent then comforts him, the parent is inadvertently reinforcing the hyperventilation. Extinction involves withdrawing the comforting response.

A child may learn to make frequent illness-oriented complaints if parents only make nurturant responses to communications which are physically oriented or illness-related. If the child's goal is nurturance and support, then physical complaints become the automatic message. For example, a 7-year-old who regularly complains of a sore throat at bedtime may simply be conveying that he needs more parental attention. In the absence of disease, frequent illness-oriented complaints may be readily treated.

The first step is to determine the goal of the complaints, for example parental attention or nurture, and then to identify other means the child uses to attain that goal, for example asking for a cuddle. A baseline frequency count is obtained of the undesirable behaviour, for example physical complaints, for a week or two. At the next session the parents are advised to: (1) consistently respond to the child's verbal request for a cuddle with immediate attention and comforting; (2) ignore physical complaints (after a cursory assessment has excluded the presence of a serious condition) *absolutely every time*, because intermittent reinforcement strongly encourages persistence of the target behaviour; (3) anticipate an early increase in physical complaints and then a gradual decrease over one to six weeks; and (4) note that once they have started ignoring physical complaints, and these have increased in frequency, a return to their former response may result in the child's physical complaints remaining at a new higher frequency. This is because starting an extinction programme and not persisting until the behaviour begins to disappear may result in the child's behaviour getting worse.

The following clinical example of behaviour modification is applicable in any setting, and the principles can be generalized to many problems. Roy, aged 13, was born with a mild meningomyelocele that had been repaired during infancy. On casual observation Roy looked well, with normal behaviour, posture and gait. One of his recurrent medical problems was urinary tract infections due to a poorly functioning (neurogenic) bladder. Roy had worn napkins/diapers all his life, although he could be dry with frequent urinary catheterizations. He had been taught to catheterize himself by age 11 years, but he and his parents infrequently performed catheterizations at home. In an effort to prevent further infection urologists had advised that the bladder be emptied six times daily by self-catheterization.

At the time of initial referral, the urologist had been unable to motivate Roy to perform the frequent self-catheterizations, and his renal function had begun to deteriorate. Other than the birth defect and its complications, Roy's development and current attainments were age-appropriate. The family consisted of the two parents, Roy and a younger sister. Father had been unemployed for four years and the family was poor. Roy had always been close to his mother but had become more involved with father since his unemployment. Roy did not respond as well to his mother's directives as he did to his father's. Mother felt guilty about Roy's defect and very sorry for him.

The following programme was devised. Roy was to catheterize himself six times a day, five days a week, and father was to document these with red checks on a calendar. On the weekend after two good weeks father was either to take Roy fishing or to the local stock-car races. The therapist explained to the family the usual course of initial success and then relapse. The programme was successful for three months and then father began to omit the rewards. Roy's old pattern of catheterization returned. The course of therapy was terminated with the family understanding that Roy could and would follow the very intrusive medical regimen if properly motivated.

Eighteen months later Roy was re-referred for treatment because his renal function had begun to deteriorate more rapidly. Major surgery would be necessary to 'save' his kidneys if his compliance did not improve. Once again a behaviour modification programme was constructed. On this occasion the therapist repeatedly emphasized the importance of the father persevering with rewards. At review two months later Roy had catheterized himself six times a day every day and father had supplied the rewards. The therapist was lavish in his praise of father.

Six months later father said that Roy had begun to feel more comfortable dry, and with an empty bladder. He also reported that Roy seemed to be getting into the habit of doing his catheterizations and rewards did not seem necessary. The treatment remained successful during the succeeding two years, with Roy receiving only personal comfort and social approval as rewards. Roy's renal function improved and surgery was avoided.

Had the programme failed yet again because of father's lack of motivation, it might have been appropriate to supplement it with tangible rewards for father as well as Roy. Behavioural techniques may fail if: (1) the programme is too complex, demanding or inconsistently applied; (2) there is inappropriate choice of rewards; (3) the parents are insufficiently motivated; (4) the behaviour required is beyond the child's developmental skills; and (5) the aims are not immediately attainable and can only be reached in smaller stages. Occasionally a 'top-up' or brief repeat programme is necessary. A useful practice manual for the behavioural treatment of children has been prepared by Herbert (1987).

7.6 PARENTAL COUNSELLING

Counselling differs from advising and behaviour modification in that the latter techniques are predominantly prescriptive, i.e. they involve one person telling another what to do, or how to do it. Counselling, in contrast, is based on listening and helping parents to explore their feelings and difficulties, as a way of resolving their problems using their own resources. One session of parental counselling is often sufficient, but sometimes it is useful to arrange for a short course of up to six sessions, at intervals varying from weekly to monthly.

A number of strategies are available within counselling, including (1) ventilation, (2) clarification, (3) encouragement, and (4) promotion of insight.

7.6.1 Ventilation

Allowing parents to unburden immediate feelings is itself therapeutic; its additional value is that it can then 'clear the way' for the calmer consideration of the problem. Acknowledging and validating such feelings enhances parental sense of worth in the same way as for children.

The mother of Emma, aged 7, was convinced that Emma's life-threatening illness was her fault because of previously having taken the contraceptive pill. No amount of reasoning and explanation convinced her otherwise, until she had spent a couple of sessions expressing her guilt and distress. The therapist's acceptance of her feelings then allowed her to consider the problem in a more rational manner.

7.6.2 Clarification

Explaining processes, discussing issues and answering questions all contribute to this process, once again allowing parents to think more clearly about a problem, and to consider the merits of different courses of action.

Wendy's parents were unable to accept that her cyclical vomiting (section 3.4) was not due to serious physical disease. The therapist put aside an additional hour, and drew diagrams to explain the psychophysiological processes, including the underlying physiological substrate. This clarification helped them to accept the appropriate treatment.

7.6.3 Encouragement

Helping parents to recognize their skills and strengths often assists them to overcome doubts and lack of confidence, and to find new and more effective ways of handling problems.

Laurie, aged 12, had refused to walk or talk for several weeks. Her parents felt demoralized and undermined. The therapist was able to point out what an excellent job they had made of bringing up their other children, and encouraged them to persevere with Laurie, using the same techniques, despite her distressing problem. With this reinforcement they started tackling the problem with renewed enthusiasm.

7.6.4 Promotion of insight

It is sometimes useful to help parents recognize why they behave in a particular way. For example, many parents repeat the pattern of parenting that they received as children, whilst others react by taking the opposite approach. Armed with such an awareness it can be easier to alter an inappropriate style.

Greg's parents had both been physically abused as children, and had avoided any sort of confrontation in their handling of their 11-year-old son. Whenever he wanted to avoid doing something he mentioned some physical complaint, and was immediately cosseted. Discussion of their own family background helped his parents recognize their inappropriate reaction, and they were able to make appropriate adjustments.

In the following example each of the above techniques has been used. Sean, aged 8, had aggressive outbursts during which he was both verbally and physically abusive to his parents and younger brother. During these episodes his parents were unable to reason with him, and afterwards he would be contrite and unable to remember why they started. His parents were convinced that there must be a physical cause, and sought repeated consultations and investigations. They were unable to take control of Sean during the outbursts, or to remonstrate with him afterwards. Their paediatrician could not convince them of the behavioural as opposed to the medical nature of the problem, and had a difficult time dissuading them from seeking a fourth opinion.

A social worker met the parents and elicited their considerable distress at the situation. She then discussed with them what made it difficult to accept the paediatrician's opinion. Sean's mother described her own childhood experiences of seeing her father's personality change from calm and easy-going to violent and abusive following a severe head injury. Sean's father recognized that his doubts related to his brother having died from a brain tumour. The therapist encouraged both parents to share their feelngs about these tragic events. She then helped them to recognize how their current attitudes stemmed from these previous unhappy experiences. In contrast they explored together how they had been able to cope with previous difficulties and, prior to the onset of these episodes, have two happy healthy children.

This counselling process, which included ventilation, clarification, encouragement and promotion of insight, enabled the parents to move from a doubting, resistant and helpless view of the problem to adopting an accepting, active and optimistic approach. They set firm and clear rules for Sean, rewarding him when he coped with stress more appropriately, and handled any tantrums by removing him from the room. The tantrums had ceased within six weeks of the commencement of counselling.

7.7 SUMMARY

Helping parents is an essential aspect of any treatment for children with physical problems. No treatment can be optimally effective unless the parents are part of the therapy team. A therapeutic alliance must be developed as a foundation for the provision of advice or counselling and the use of behaviour modification techniques. Consistency between the parents and over time is an essential component.

Where fundamental problems exist in the marriage these are best tackled in a separate context, and we discuss marital therapy in the next chapter.

CHAPTER 8

Family Therapy

Accidents will occur in the best-regulated families
Charles Dickens (Mr Micawber in David Copperfield)

GUIDE FOR THE READER

In this chapter we provide an overview of what is at present an increasingly popular and apparently valuable mode of therapy. We do not offer a manual of how to do it, but instead give several illustrations of different techniques. The novice will want to pursue some of the references and hopefully learn some of the skills, whilst the experienced family therapist will want to comment on our omissions and criticize our prejudices!

8.1 INTRODUCTION

Family therapy differs from all individual therapies in its focus on the whole family as opposed to the individual. Regardless of the origins of the disorder the family therapist is concerned to understand the complex interaction between that disorder and the family.

Although there is often a tendency to view the family negatively, i.e. the family has caused and is perpetuating the problem, therapy tends to be more successful if a positive view is taken: 'we don't know the cause of this problem but let's find a way to help the family to cope with or overcome it.'

There is no universally accepted theory of family functioning but there is agreement about the family's basic tasks: the provision of emotional bonds and relationships, a secure base, and models of behaviours and attitudes, the enhancement of life experiences, the shaping of behaviour and the establishment of a communication network (Lidz, 1968). The family is the main learning context for individual behaviour, thoughts and feelings (Satir, 1978) and it is in this context that family therapists view the origin or maintenance of problems. Many different ideas have contributed to the assessment and treatment of families (Bentovim *et al.*, 1987a; Lask, 1989), and in this chapter we attempt to relate such thinking to the application of family therapy in childhood illness.

Central to our thinking are the interactions (1) between family members and (2) between the family and the illness. These concepts are illustrated in Figures 8.1–8.4. Figure 8.1 shows the linear sequence in which a child's illness causes the mother to worry. However (the mother's) anxiety can be stressful for the child and can exacerbate the illness (Figure 8.2). Thus there is more than cause and effect—there is an interaction within the dyad. Other family members are invariably involved in similar interactions, as shown in Figure 8.3—a triadic interaction. The irritated father can have an adverse effect on the child or vice versa, and so a vicious cycle is established.

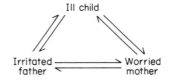

Figure 8.1 Cause and effect in a dyad

Figure 8.2 Dyadic interaction

Figure 8.3 Triadic interaction

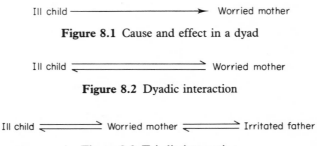

Figure 8.4 Vicious cycle

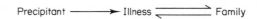

Figure 8.5 Illness aetiology and maintenance

In addition, it should not be forgotten that what initiates an illness may be quite different from what maintains or aggravates it (Figure 8.5). The initial cause may still be present, or lost in the mists of time. Attention now has to be paid to secondary factors, which all too frequently relate to family dysfunction.

Before further considering family dysfunction, we should not lose sight of family strengths. Families which satisfactorily fulfil their basic tasks are likely to be able to cope well with an ill child, and are unlikely to have a child who persistently expresses feelings through physical complaints. A well-functioning family is manifested by: (1) firm but not rigid parenting, that is consistent over time and between the parents; (2) the ability to make decisions, solve problems and resolve conflicts; (3) open and clear communications; (4) the ability to express and respond appropriately to everyday needs; and (5) respect for each person's individuality and the children's need for increasing independence.

8.2 FAMILY DYSFUNCTION

A family is dysfunctional when: (1) parenting is lax, rigid or inconsistent; (2) there is an inability to make decisions, solve problems or resolve conflicts; (3) communications are indirect and/or unclear; (4) there is an inability to express and respond appropriately to everyday needs and emotions; and (5) there is no respect for each person's individuality and the children's need for increasing independence.

8.2.1 Inadequate and/or inconsistent parenting

Parenting should be neither unduly lax nor rigid. Laxity does not allow children to develop appropriate degrees of internal control, whilst too rigid control either prevents the development of flexibility or may lead to a reactive rebellion and stubbornness. A child may experience a warm response to tears from one parent but not the other; or one parent may allow a child to watch television during the meal whilst the other may forbid it. When parents are inconsistent, with the mother having one set of rules or responses and the father another, the contradictions eventually create confusion and distress.

Inconsistency may also occur over time; i.e. a particular set of rules may apply on one day, for example the children should not argue with their parents, whilst on the next a vigorous exchange of opinion may be allowed, or even encouraged. Parents also need to make decisions, solve problems and resolve conflicts as well as allowing themselves time for each other. These everyday tasks are usually carried out spontaneously and without difficulty, but some families seem unable to complete them, with resulting indecisiveness, disorganization, and sometimes tension and resentment.

Children very commonly get caught up in marital conflict, either by taking sides, being asked to take sides, modelling parental conflict by arguing among themselves, or developing problems that cause the parents to come together in their concern or resentment. Somatization is a frequent response to this process of 'triangulation' (Lask, 1982b).

A tendency to laxity, and making allowances, is common in families of sick children. In general such an approach is unhelpful and encourages the development of behavioural patterns that later cause distress. All children need to learn internal controls. These are achieved by experiencing appropriate control by parents or other significant adults, and by appropriate behaviour being modelled within the family. If a child with chronic illness is allowed to have his way most of the time, then he cannot develop a mode of coping when he cannot have his way. Further, he is at greater risk of not complying with treatment.

8.2.2 Communication problems

Many different forms of communication dysfunction exist.

8.2.2.1 Inhibited communication

Little is said, there are prolonged periods of silence, problems are neither discussed nor resolved, and secrets abound.

8.2.2.2 Excess communication

There is little silence and much noise; family members frequently interrupt each other, fail to listen, or make long speeches whose true meaning is difficult to grasp.

8.2.2.3 Non-congruent communication

Normally there is congruence between what is said and how it is said; a sad piece of information is accompanied by a sad facial expression and tone of voice. If, however, the same sad message is delivered with a smile, the true meaning of the communication is blurred. This form of incongruence occurs occasionally in most families, but if repeated frequently the effect is confusing and demoralizing.

8.2.2.4 Displaced communication

Thoughts and feelings are expressed by behaviour or physical symptoms (somatization) rather than words. A child who is fearful of attending school may have morning headaches or panic attacks rather than openly talking about the fears. The parents may respond to the headaches as if these represented a serious physical disorder, and a pattern of illness behaviour is soon established.

8.2.2.5 Deviant communication

These other forms of dysfunctional communication include the presence of 'the switchboard operator', via whom all communications are channelled (this person may be known as 'the family spokesman'), 'mind readers' who assume (and are often convinced) that they know exactly what others are thinking and therefore speak for them, and 'nebulous communication' in which the point is never reached or messages are too vague to be understood.

Problems are liable to occur in families where any of these dysfunctional communications occur frequently.

8.2.3 Abnormal emotional expression and responsiveness

When family members can identify, express, accept and share painful feelings, each person feels supported and understood. With illness, however, it is not uncommon for there to be an uneven distribution of emotions, or an inability to respond appropriately. For example, the parents may feel sad and the child angry; or the mother and child sad, and the father and sibling resentful; or the mother guilty, the child sad and the father denying. Any combination is possible and potentially problematic.

For example, Greg's father responded to his seven-year-old son's depression at having a leg amputated for a malignant disease, by blaming the very doctors who were trying to help for insisting on such a radical treatment. Greg could only sit and cry during his father's outbursts. His mother in consequence felt especially protective and would cancel radiotherapy sessions.

Annie, aged 12, also had a malignant disease, and her father could not cope with his own distress. After she had completed a course of treatment he held a surprise party at which he announced that Annie was cured. His wife was furious, and Annie was so embarrassed she ran from the room. Father's denial had caused turmoil.

Denial is a common way of attempting to ward off feelings of sadness, anger, guilt and vulnerability. A mother might, for example, see her asthmatic son playing football, and think to herself: 'He looks so healthy, surely he doesn't need all those medicines.' This might form the rationale for her lax approach to treatment, with subsequent exacerbations of the asthma.

The problems associated with sad parents and denying chronically ill adolescents can be severe and recalcitrant. Denial of mortality and vulnerability is a very common posture among healthy teenagers, and the phenomenon is found among chronically ill adolescents. The benefits of this state for the adolescent are psychological and social. For example, diabetic adolescents who deny their condition may leave all the responsibility for the insulin injections, dietary restrictions, regimented exercise and monitoring to their parents. They are then free from worry about the disease, and can participate in coke and pizza parties freely with their peers. The sad parents, feeling sorry for themselves and their children, are unable to provide the necessary firmness and structure to ensure their child's health.

Rationalization is closely linked to denial. Janine, 14, had suffered from asthma for six years. She was frightened that she might die during an attack, and was also concerned about her mother's increasing ill health. Her parents could not cope with her fears, which reminded them of their own concerns. They dismissed her as a 'worrier', and instead of acknowledging her distress coaxed her into laughter. Janine responded by attempting to hide her fears, leading to persisting and heightened levels of emotional arousal, and subsequent poor control of her illness. The parental rationalization was exacerbating the problem.

8.2.4 Over- and under-involvement

Relationships vary along a continuum of involvement from over-involved (enmeshed) to distant (disengaged). A typical, but normal, enmeshment occurs between a mother and her newborn baby. This relationship is almost exclusive of others, and is generally seen as appropriate. As the baby grows so a slow loosening of this tightly bonded relationship should occur, so that separation and individuation may gradually happen. As children grow, their interests, needs and relationships change, and parents have to allow for this whilst still ensuring their health and safety. Problems commonly arise from over-close relationships at crucial developmental stages, such as separation anxiety in toddlers, and school refusal in mid-childhood and adolescence. Over-involved and over-protective relationships are understandably common in illness (Chapter 4), and often exacerbate the problem.

Jason was 13 when he suffered a seizure for no obvious reason. His divorced mother was terrified that he might suffer another, and even die during it. In consequence she refused to leave him unattended, slept beside him, accompanied him to the bathroom and kept him away from school. Although he had no further seizures he gradually lost his independence, and at the time of referral to a psychiatrist six months later was unable or unwilling to do anything for himself. He was mute, immobile, and refused to swallow anything. Intracranial pathology had been excluded. There was no recurrence of the seizure, the cause of which remained unidentified. The other symptoms seemed to be a direct response to the enmeshment with his mother, and only resolved spontaneously on admission to hospital with an enforced separation.

Distant relationships are characterized by considerable degrees of separateness and unresponsiveness, lack of concern and restricted communication. A father may, for example, have wanted a son after having two daughters, and when the third daughter is born he might take no interest in her, and allow a persisting separateness to develop. Such children may develop a poor self-image, behavioural problems or excessive adolescent rebelliousness. Although not as common as over-involvement, such relationships also occur in association with illness.

Ahmed was 8 when he developed a condition which involved the onset of premature puberty. His father, perhaps understandably, found this very difficult to tolerate, and distanced himself to the point that he avoided Ahmed as much as possible. He took no part in his medical care and showed very little interest in his achievements. Ahmed became increasingly depressed by his very obvious differences from his peer group and lack of acceptance by his father. Eventually he refused to take his medication, saying that he would prefer to die, with consequent deterioration of his primary disorder. Once more an unhealthy relationship had contributed to the exacerbation of illness.

In many marriages there is a considerable distance between the spouses, usually associated with marital conflict. In such instances the father frequently distances himself from the family and becomes relatively uninvolved (the 'peripheral father'). The eldest child may then suffer the adverse effects of being used by the mother as an alternative spouse or parent ('parental child'). The consequent stresses are often difficult for the child to tolerate. Involvement of a child in marital conflict, 'triangulation', has been discussed earlier and is even more problematic (Lask B., 1982b).

8.2.5 Family medical myths

A family myth is a well-integrated belief shared by all family members, which goes unchallenged by everyone involved, in spite of the illogicality or unreality of the views held (Ferreira, 1963). Examples might be 'We never feel cross with each other'; 'Feeling sad is a weakness'; 'We are always a hundred per cent honest with each other.' Family myths are often defences against unpalatable ideas or facts.

Family medical myths are false or distorted health beliefs, serving a similar purpose (Hardwick, 1989). 'Father must not be upset because he might get a heart attack'; 'Granny had a stroke because you were naughty'; 'Johnny had a hole in the heart because I worked during the pregnancy.' Hardwick has noted that

> Family medical myths commonly present during therapy and can stifle the natural capacity for change. They are often constructed around medical or behaviour problems, exaggeration or denial of illness and handicap, and guilt regarding cause. Some myths result from outdated or unsubstantiated beliefs held by professionals; for example that autism and schizophrenia can be caused by parental handling and communication dysfunction respectively. Medical myths are common in childhood; for example 'I'm ill because I have been naughty' or 'Mummy is sick because I fight a lot with my brother'.

8.3 CONTEXT OF THERAPY

Family therapy is practised in a wide variety of settings (Lask, 1987c), including family practice, social service agencies, paediatric departments and adult and child psychiatric departments. Therapists may come from any of the mental health professions and would normally have had a training in family therapy. They may work singly or as a team of co-therapists. In the latter case two

therapists may work together in the room with the family, or one may work
directly with the family, whilst the other observes through closed-circuit video
or a one-way screen. This distancing allows one therapist to remain detached
and more objective. In whatever form, co-therapy is a valuable mode of
working, providing the therapists are able to work effectively as a team,
identify, discuss and resolve differences, and complement each other's skills.

Most family therapists make use of video to enhance their work. Reviewing a
family therapy session assists the therapist in understanding better the complexities of family interaction and the effect of therapeutic interventions. If the
time is available it is always useful to review a previous session. Even watching
five minutes of a videotape often reveals previously hidden patterns, and assists
in devising further therapeutic strategies.

Every effort should be made to ensure that the whole family attends. Missing
members may reflect family resistance, and are very likely to impede the
effectiveness of any interventions. Sometimes one session of family therapy is
sufficient, but in complex situations up to ten or even more meetings may be
necessary, held at weekly or fortnightly intervals.

8.4 TECHNIQUES OF THERAPY

There are as many ways of treating families as there are family therapists, and
there is no shortage of handbooks on the subject of family therapy in different
contexts and different styles. Amongst the most relevant to the topic of
childhood illness is the excellent (although misnamed) *Psychosomatic Families*
by Minuchin *et al.* (1978). In this section we have outlined techniques we find
useful, some learned from colleagues, others our own. Underlying these is the
aim, not necessarily of understanding or focusing on the symptom or illness, but
rather understanding and helping the family. Indeed, a specific focus on illness
may detract from major underlying issues that have caused or are aggravating
the illness.

Laura, 11, had a two-year history of anorexia nervosa. Her father, a trade
union leader, was a highly argumentative man who attacked anyone in
authority. His wife and children worked hard at keeping the peace by not
arguing with him. Whenever the family therapist attempted to explore these
issues Laura's father would criticize the style of work and bring the discussions
back to her illness and its management. The therapist adopted the same style of
coping as the rest of the family and acquiesced, allowing each session to focus on
the illness rather than the family dysfunction.

8.4.1 The structure

As with many tasks, careful preparation and the appropriate tools make a
substantial difference. The importance of forming a therapeutic alliance with
the family has been emphasized in Chapter 5, and is illustrated by the case

example above. A comfortable room, with age-appropriate play material for children, aids communication, whilst a clear structure for the meeting allows the time to be used to the optimum. We tell the family how long the meeting will last, and advise them of any intention we have to take breaks in the middle. 'Taking a break' is a common practice in family therapy, and allows the therapist 'space' to think about what is happening, to escape from the often intense emotional atmosphere, and to consult with a colleague who may be viewing through closed-circuit video or a one-way screen.

We structure the meeting to allow ten minutes or so at the start to discuss issues specifically relating to the illness, such as investigations, treatment and progress. All such details have then been dealt with before the 'therapy' starts. Without such a structure the therapy is often blocked by illness-related matters being raised during the meeting, sometimes as a defence against painful family issues, and at other times as a genuine and justified need for information. Non-medical family therapists should use the same technique—the family needs the opportunity. Such therapists can, if necessary, act as a go-between, and help the family formulate questions which they may find hard to ask the doctor. Often it helps families to 'unload' feelings about the illness.

8.4.2 Formulation and focus

These should always guide the therapy. The formulation is the family therapy equivalent of a diagnosis but is considerably more comprehensive. It usually consists of a statement which summarizes the key components of family interaction, and seeks to explain the presenting problem and its maintenance. The focus arises from the formulation and is that aspect of family interaction that the therapist considers most useful to concentrate upon.

Jenny, aged 12, had a six-month history of increasing fatigue, weakness, loss of appetite and headaches. At the time of admission to hospital she was no longer eating or walking. No organic cause could be found for her symptoms. The family, consisting of Jenny, her sister Christine, 14, and parents, both aged 38, was characterized by restricted communication, considerable tension, a failure to respond to distress, an absence of warmth and a tendency to blame Jenny, saying that if only she were well there would be no problems. The family tended to diffuse tension by joking. Jenny's symptoms appeared to be an expression of her inability to communicate her painful feelings, and the family's tendency to respond only to physical rather than emotional suffering. The therapist chose to focus on the family's difficulty in expressing and responding to distress.

8.4.3 Agreement and responsibility

Once the formulation and focus are clear, it is essential to get the family's agreement to work on these issues. Without their consent therapy is likely to fail, for teamwork is essential. If the family do not agree with the therapist's view much time is wasted in argument and resistance (an excellent guide to 'mastering resistance' has been written by Anderson and Stewart, 1983). We find it helpful to take a kind but firm line at such times, stating that this is how we see the situation. We recognize that each person may have a different view, but point out that we can only help from our perspective. We acknowledge the family's right to seek help elsewhere, and if they are very resistant we might encourage them to seek another opinion. We point out, however, that meanwhile one person at least in the family is in distress and we are willing to help the family find solutions.

This links to the locus of responsibility. Many families seek help, expecting a 'medical' solution—a drug or other simple remedy, or at least something the therapist will do to make things better. Whilst clearly therapists have a responsibility to help their clients find solutions to their problems, it is a shared responsibility. The family have to work as hard as the therapist, and the therapist must help the family to take their share.

8.4.4 Here and now

Given all those provisos we find it useful to work in the 'here and now', i.e. concentrating on what is happening in the room now (process), as well as what the family says (content). We consider present functioning to be as important as past history. It is rarely that we can be certain why a problem has arisen, but we can often see what is keeping it going.

We encourage enactment of the family difficulties—directing the family to discuss problems here and now. We ask the family members to talk to each other as much as to us, so that we can help identify and overcome unhelpful modes of communication and recognize and tackle other forms of dysfunction.

Riaz, aged 8, had suffered intense headaches for several months; his father had lost status since immigrating, and was currently unemployed and was himself experiencing fatigue and headache. Whenever the therapist mentioned father's plight, Riaz would close his eyes and tell his father of his terrible pains. This served to distract from father's situation and gave father an important role.

The parents of Peter, aged 12, referred because of recurrent abdominal pain, showed an inability to deal with disagreements. When the therapist encouraged them to work out how to resolve their conflicts Peter immediately doubled up and complained of tummy-ache. The therapist was able to help Peter's parents recognize this pattern and work out how to overcome it.

8.4.5 Space and position

A further advantage of 'here and now' work is the use of the family's seating arrangements. The identified patient often sits between the parents, seeming to indicate his role as buffer or mediator. Sometimes a child and one parent sit very close to one another whilst other family members are much further apart. Alliances may be demonstrated by mother and one child sitting close together, and father and another child sitting closely, but some distance away from the other two. A third (and perhaps the referred) child may sit alone.

James, aged 13, had poorly controlled asthma, and his brother Michael, aged 15, suffered, like his father, from migraine. James and his mother pulled their chairs closer together, and she would stroke his hair and squeeze his hand whilst the others sat isolated. This observation allowed the therapist to restructure the family, by asking the parents to sit together and, opposite them, the two brothers. Everyone except the mother felt more comfortable. The therapist asked her to tell her husband what she wanted him to do that would help, and this led to an outburst from her about how neglected by him she felt. He in turn complained that she never seemed to have time for him as she was so involved with James. She replied that James needed this attention because of his asthma. The therapist pointed out the vicious cycle and advised the parents to ensure that they had some time alone together most evenings. James' asthma improved and the frequency of the migraines diminished.

8.4.6 Parenting

Where parents demonstrate a lack of consistency, either over time or between each other, we advise them of the importance of their team-work. We encourage them to sit together, to discuss issues now, and to find agreement when this has previously been absent. We coach them in preventing intrusions or detouring by the children, and point out inappropriate alliances across generations. Most importantly, we encourage parents to be firmly in charge and help them towards the identification and acknowledgement of problems and conflicts, so that firm decisions can be made, problems tackled and conflicts resolved.

Whilst all this may sound directive to the point of dictatorial, we see it as being authoritative rather than authoritarian. It is perfectly possible to combine such firmness with empathy and even humour.

Amy, aged 11, had been referred because of persistent limb pains. She infuriated Alan, aged 9, by bossing both him and her adoring parents. They sat back and allowed Amy to attempt to control Alan's aggressive responses. The therapist had failed to help the parents take control, and eventually pointed out to the family that Amy was being allowed to act as a parent to her brother and her parents. He then jokingly asked Amy how it felt to be an 11-year-old-grandmother. The parents then seemed more able to understand the significance of what was happening and to take charge. Amy's pains soon disappeared. (A common principle of family therapy is to restore the family hierarchy, with parents in charge of children, and grandparents available but peripheral. Where this hierarchy is disturbed, families usually develop problems.)

8.4.7 Communication training

'Here and now' work allows for the recognition of the various forms of communication dysfunction (see section 8.2.2).

Sharon, aged 8, complained of thumping in the chest that kept her awake and for which no organic cause could be found. Father acted as a spokesman for the family, and regardless of whom the therapist addressed a question, it was he that answered. He also spoke on behalf of all family members, seeming to know what they were thinking and feeling. When challenged about this father became quite distressed and Sharon, rushing to his rescue said 'But he knows me better than anyone else does.'

In such circumstances the therapist may have to insist that each person talks for himself or herself, and block attempts of one family member to talk about others in their presence. Instead they are encouraged to ask questions of each other, such as 'Are you worried?' or clearly label the statement as an opinion, for example 'I think you are worried' or 'You seem to be worried', rather than 'He is worried' or 'You are worried.'

In families where there is excessive communication it is often helpful to insist that only one person speaks at a time; the therapist can gently remind the family of his or her weakness in being only able to listen to one person at a time. Interruptions are initially blocked by the therapist whilst family members learn how to ignore them. In families where members speak for too long, so that others stop listening or lose the point, each person is asked to say only one sentence at a time, with no more than about fifteen words. At first they find this very difficult and tend to break the rules, but with gentle insistence from the therapist they eventually manage. The outcome is often that many previously unspoken or unheard points come to the fore.

Families with inhibited or displaced communication need a far gentler approach. The therapist acknowledges painful feelings, gently encourages each person to speak, and attempts to 'guess' unspoken thoughts or feelings. Children's play and drawings are taken as important communications and may be used as a therapeutic technique.

Bernice, aged 8, who had been failing to thrive, drew her family looking miserable and separate. The therapist asked each family member to draw their view of the family, and then to draw how they would like the family to be. This depressed and inhibited group suddenly came to life and had, for them, a relatively animated discussion about their different pictures.

'Sculpting' (Duhl *et al.*, 1973) is another technique of value for families where communication is inhibited. Family members are moulded during the therapy session into positions symbolizing their actual relationships, as seen by one or more family members. The sculpture provides a perspective of family relationships, not available in words.

John, aged 7, portrayed his 11-year-old sister Rosie who had anorexia nervosa in a tight embrace with her father, whilst he and his mother looked on from the far end of the room.

Non-congruent communications should be gently pointed out, and the importance of these explained.

Six-year-old Paul's parents were concerned about his defiance, which included breaking the diet he required for his coeliac disease. The therapist noticed that whenever he was told off by his parents they would smile, and in consequence he never took what they said seriously. Both parents explained that they had had a very strict upbringing and did not want to be so severe with Paul. They needed considerable convincing that Paul's non-compliance with his diet was a response to this.

8.4.8 Learning about emotions

There are many similarities in the management of dysfunctional communication and inappropriate handling of emotions. When emotional expression is restricted or displaced the same techniques used for inhibited or displaced communication are of value. 'Emotional incontinence' (the continuous outpouring of emotions) does not respond to advice to try and control feelings. Whilst such behaviour is frequently a characteristic of a particular temperament, it is usually also a reaction to a lack of support and understanding by other family members.

Wendy, aged 14, had suffered seizures since infancy. Her mother was terrified of these and would talk non-stop to anyone who would listen about how upsetting they were. Wendy, who often heard these outbursts, blamed herself for her mother's distress, and her own anxiety at upsetting her mother may well have precipitated further attacks. The therapist encouraged Wendy's father, who was so irritated by his wife's outbursts that he usually left the room, to stay and comfort her, and to encourage her to cry on his shoulder. Once she felt that her burden was shared she became less anxious, and Wendy's seizures correspondingly reduced in frequency.

An over-reaction with excessive concern to the point of intrusiveness is just as harmful. Twelve-year-old Darren's mother was so concerned that he might go into a diabetic coma if he was upset, that she accompanied him everywhere, including into the school building, much to the delight of his peers. She tested his urine four times a day and monitored everything he ate. She organized the rest of the family to avoid any distress. No amount of rational discussion would convince her that she was impeding her son's development and ability to care for himself. It took several hours of patient exploration of her own background to help her bring to consciousness a deeply suppressed guilt, with regard to her own father's death from a heart attack, following a marital row about her, when she was 11 years old. The therapist advised that she have some therapy for herself, and in the meantime that the father take responsibility for Darren's diabetic control, knowing that he would allow Darren more freedom. It took several weeks before father learned how to support his wife without allowing her to take over.

A contrasting reaction is that of denial and rationalization. Denise, aged 13, had been admitted to hospital sixteen times in the previous year because of poor diabetic control. A family interview revealed that whenever she got upset her parents joked her out of it, without listening to what was bothering her. They described her as 'just a worrier', and so failed to recognize her intense anxiety that she might die. The consequent emotional arousal precipitated episodes of hyperglycaemia. The therapist prescribed a worry time for half an hour each day, during which they were to encourage her to talk about her worries without making any effort to reassure her, cheer her up, or rationalize her concerns. She in turn had to say as much as she could about her worries. There was a remarkable improvement, with only one hospital admission in the next eighteen months.

8.4.9 Re-editing medical myths

Hardwick (1989) has written very clearly on this topic. He suggests that it is always worth trying to challenge a myth directly—'It is not helpful for you to avoid upsetting Darren; his diabetes won't get worse if you upset him, and anyhow he has to learn to cope with being upset by others; the whole world won't protect him like you do.' Such challenges may work in 'young' myths but did not in Darren's case, as the beliefs were too deeply entrenched. Other techniques involve: (1) emphasizing and developing strengths that make the myth redundant, for example sending Darren to a summer camp for diabetics to show how well he can cope; (2) engineering conflict so that the family members can experience survival despite distress; (3) encouraging parents to take control and handle a difficult child who happens also to have an illness, as if he was simply a difficult child—'Greg needs to know that just because he has a kidney disease he can't be rude and defiant'; (4) promoting normal behaviour despite illness—'Okay, so Jim has a bout of bowel disease and that's likely to stay with him, but he still has to go to school. If he stays off school in case he gets diarrhoea, he'll never learn that it is safe to go out anywhere, and he will end up a prisoner'; (5) working with the wider system—advising doctors to stop further investigations of unexplained or poorly controlled illness; arranging for unnecessary medication or unhelpful labels to be withdrawn; reducing overprotectiveness; stopping or preventing the medical treatment of somatization.

8.4.10 Genograms (or family trees)

The construction of a family tree by the family with the therapist's guidance can help the family understand, and where necessary overcome, such transgenerational influences as patterns, styles, customs, ceremonies, secrets, myths and dysfunctions which determine the uniqueness of the family (Lieberman, 1979).

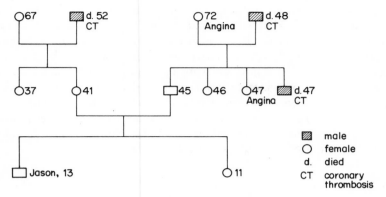

Figure 8.6 Jason's family tree

The origins and maintenance of illness are often only fully understood by following the patterns of illness through the generations. Figure 8.6 illustrates Jason's family tree, and the reason for his previously unexplained six months history of chest pain becomes painfully clear.

8.4.11 Family circles

This technique differs from a family tree in that it is a portrayal of any individual's perception of his or her current family relationships (Thrower *et al.*, 1982; Tomson, 1983).

Figure 8.7 illustrates how 14-year-old Gerald portrayed his family. His knee joints were hyperextensible and were liable to ache after exercise, but this could

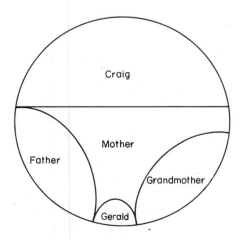

Figure 8.7 Gerald's family circle

not explain the six-year history of severe knee pains, for which no other organic cause could be found. His brother Craig (now 18) had been a school refuser since he was 12, and for the last four years had been a defiant, argumentative and disruptive teenager, who managed to get his own way by threats and rudeness. His parents gave in to his demands, and what little time mother had left she gave to her own mother, who lived nearby. Gerald only got parental attention when his knees hurt. His family circle clearly demonstrates his sense of deprivation in a family dominated by his brother. Gerald had been unable to describe this with words. Circles can be drawn by each family member and can if desired include friends, hobbies, school or work, and so on.

8.4.12 Metaphors (see also Chapter 9)

These are stories, anecdotes, actions or objects that the therapist can use to communicate ideas. Their value is in being able to reach affective components of the individual, or family relationships, that might be too strongly resisted to be reachable. Metaphors can be used for decreasing resistance, suggesting solutions to problems, increasing motivation and helping mobilize positive resources. The range of use of metaphor is enormous and is excellently illustrated by Barker (1985).

A simple example might arise from the case of Gerald (above). The therapist had noted how unable he was to express his anger with his brother, and with his parents for allowing Craig to dominate. The therapist, almost as if thinking aloud, mused 'I suppose it would really hurt if you or your parents were to kick Craig out.' This led to a family discussion about the rights and wrongs of such an action, with Gerald for the first time expressing his ambivalence about Craig. At no time during the session were Gerald's pains discussed, but the metaphorical translation of his symptoms as a previously unexpressed anger minimized their impact.

8.5 MARITAL AND FAMILY THERAPY

We perceive marital (or couple) therapy as a form of family therapy which focuses on the marriage (or couple's relationship) rather than other aspects of family life. It is important to re-emphasize the difference between the parental and marital subsystems. Although usually consisting of the same two people, the functions of the two subsystems differ. The parental subsystem is concerned with all aspects of child care, whilst the marital subsystem is concerned with the spouse relationship. Parenting issues are discussed fully in Chapter 7, and can be dealt with in the context of parental counselling, when the parents are seen alone, or during family therapy in the presence of the children. The value of the latter is that the therapist can note how children may attempt to undermine their parents' competence and effectiveness. 'Here and now' strategies can then be devised and put into practice to help the parents overcome the problem.

It is totally inappropriate, however, to discuss marital issues in front of the children. In so doing the therapist is in danger of embarrassing and undermining the parents. A more appropriate sequence when parenting and marital issues seem to be relevant to the presenting problem is to deal with parenting issues in the family context and to offer marital therapy later.

Susan, aged 9, had a three-year history of headache and vomiting that appeared to be a manifestation of school phobia. She had been unable to attend school for more than two weeks per term since starting school. During the family assessment she consistently interrupted her parents, criticized them and argued with much of what they said. She frequently sided with one parent against the other. It was clear that there was considerable marital conflict, parental inconsistency and that Susan was in control of her parents.

The therapist decided to focus initially on parental competence and effectiveness, and asked them to work together on a plan for Susan's return to school. Whenever her parents started discussing the topic, Susan interrupted, initially with questions, then angry criticisms, and eventually screaming. As the therapist taught the parents not to give in to her interruptions, and to negotiate with rather than criticize each other, so she escalated the intensity of her interruptions. Each parent kept turning to the therapist for support for their view, and advice on how to handle Susan, and he responded by affirming their need to reach a decision. As they approached this point Susan's screaming reached a crescendo and suddenly she vomited. Her mother turned, almost triumphantly, to the therapist and asked 'How can we send her to school when that's what happens?' He responded by making it clear that the vomiting was one more attempt to control her parents and that they still had to get her to school.

At the next session, much to the therapist's surprise, they had succeeded in returning Susan to school, and she had settled well. They continued to blame each other for many of their problems, but were able to manage more effectively Susan's rudeness and complaints. The therapist suggested at this point that it might be useful to have some meetings with the couple to discuss their relationship. They eagerly accepted this offer and in the next meeting poured out an enormous number of complaints about each other.

Four marital therapy sessions were held, during which the work focused on the sense that each partner had that the other was unappreciative and unsupportive. Eventually the couple stated that they had gained enough for them to carry on without further help. Follow-up for several years has revealed that Susan has remained well, and the parents are more accepting of each other's faults, and are getting on far better.

The focus in marital therapy depends upon the underlying difficulties, but commonly it concerns poor or dysfunctional communication, inability to resolve conflicts, or deeper issues relating to the partner's own childhood experiences and how these interfere with current functioning. Ables and Brandsma (1977) offer a helpful guide to the intricacies of marital (or couple) therapy. In the context of ill children the key points are to help the parents to function as a team, and to restore appropriate hierarchies, before embarking, separately, on marital therapy. Although often overlooked, it is also essential to obtain an agreement to work on these issues.

8.6 INDICATIONS AND CONTRAINDICATIONS

The effectiveness of family therapy is difficult to evaluate because of the methodological complexities (Frude, 1980; Gale, 1985). Nonetheless a comprehensive review of outcome studies suggests an average improvement rate of 73% (Gurman and Kniskern, 1981). Elsewhere we have reviewed those childhood conditions in which family therapy seems valuable (Lask, 1987c): (1) physical disorders in which psychological factors play an important part in causing or aggravating the problems—for example, asthma, diabetes, epilepsy, recurrent abdominal pain and anorexia nervosa; (2) physical disorders in which, although psychological factors may not be maintaining the problem, there are adverse psychological sequelae—for example, congenital heart disease, cystic fibrosis, chronic renal disease and malignant disease; (3) behavioural and emotional problems such as school refusal, separation anxiety or other phobias, soiling, and difficult and disruptive behaviour; (4) child abuse and neglect.

The main contraindication to family therapy is when the family refuses help, or the problems are firmly located in the marriage, in which case marital therapy would be indicated. This should not be offered, however, until the child(ren) embroiled in the marital conflict has been detriangulated (see section 8.2.1).

We always offer a family assessment as an essential part of the full assessment of the problem, and family therapy unless it is contraindicated or an alternative therapy is seen as being of more value (Chapter 9). It is perfectly possible to combine therapies when this is indicated; for example, a child has a needle phobia but the family also has problems. In such an instance a desensitization programme (Chapter 7) for the phobia, plus a course of family therapy, would be appropriate.

8.7 SUMMARY

(1) Family therapy differs from individual therapies in its focus on the family rather than the individual.
(2) There is no universally accepted theory of family functioning, but a 'good enough' family will be able to carry out positively such basic tasks as the

provision of emotional bonds and relationships, a secure base, models of behaviour and a communication network.

(3) All families have strengths and all families have problems.

(4) Family therapy aims to utilize the family strengths to overcome problems.

(5) There are very many different styles of therapy, none proven to be better than others, and therapists should develop techniques with which they feel comfortable and which appear to be helpful.

CHAPTER 9

Individual Therapies

It should be noted that children at play are not playing about; their games should be seen as their most serious activity. Montaigne; Essais xxiii, *1588*

GUIDE FOR THE READER

Whilst the aims of this chapter are serious, we hope we have shown that at least some of the individual work done with children can be fun. To engage a child's interest and motivation a variety of techniques may be necessary, and we describe several that we find useful, drawn from various schools of thought and practice. Indications, limitations, and clinical and practical applications are enlivened with clinical examples, chosen to infuse a strong dose of reality.

9.1 INTRODUCTION

There are available a wide range of individual techniques for helping children with the psychological components of illness. Whilst these may differ substantially in style, they are all based on fundamental concepts.

(1) Understanding a child's predicament and accepting the feelings as perfectly reasonable provides emotional support for, and validation of, the child as an individual worthy of respect.

(2) Many adults inhibit the child's expression of angry, sad or other painful feelings, for example 'Don't get angry with me', 'Big boys don't cry', etc. The consequent feelings of guilt, badness or unworthiness exacerbate the pre-existing problem. Permitting and encouraging children to express painful feelings in socially acceptable ways enhances their sense of well-being.

(3) Helping children change their perspective on a problem often enhances coping. For example, a child with persistent pain in the legs is encouraged to focus on other parts of the body which are pain-free. Similarly, a child who is preoccupied with and distressed by problems with reading, can be helped to identify skills in other subjects or pursuits.

(4) Children benefit from gaining control over a difficult situation, whether it is by thoughts, play or action. A child who is terrified by injections, for example, can gain control by pretend play, such as giving injections to a doll figure.

(5) Finding something to be hopeful about is often highly therapeutic. A child demoralized by illness can be helped to cope by active consideration of how life will be after recovery. Where permanent handicap exists, focusing on existing skills and potentials may balance despair. It is necessary, however, to allow the expression of distress (see (1) above).

(6) Working through painful experiences is also therapeutic. For example, remembering and talking about the good times with a lost loved one, as well as expressing the pain and despair associated with the loss, helps the child eventually to overcome the distress. Remembering a traumatic experience but changing perspective is also beneficial. For example, a child can be encouraged to recall a particular event by looking in on it, and seeing himself in the picture (a view not previously taken). He is then asked to talk about the positive ways he thought and behaved, so altering the negative perspective. Finally the traditional psychoanalytic technique of focusing on the therapist/child relationship can be used to help children work through painful and traumatic experiences.

9.2 THE CONTEXT FOR INDIVIDUAL THERAPY

A number of points require consideration. Privacy is essential. Few children can discuss intimate and painful topics when there is a danger of being overheard. Ideally such interviews should be held in a quiet and comfortable room, without the possibility of interruptions by telephone or knocks on the door. The room should be well equipped with age-appropriate materials such as toys and drawing materials. For older children drawing materials may still be acceptable, and it is always useful to have something to fiddle with such as playdough or other modelling material.

Meetings should be at regular intervals, preferably the same time and day(s) each week, and for the same length of time. Younger children may find 30–40 minutes enough, whilst 50 minutes is usually sufficient for adolescents.

Clearly it is not always possible to fulfil these conditions, especially if a child is in hospital. Nonetheless the therapist should attempt to fulfil them as much as possible. The length of individual therapy is determined by the particular technique chosen; for example, psychotherapy may last for a year or more, whilst other techniques may require only one or two sessions.

9.3 ESTABLISHING A THERAPEUTIC RELATIONSHIP

Once the decision to use an individual therapy has been made (this is best left until completion of a couple of individual sessions), the therapist's first task is to construct a good therapeutic relationship. To succeed it is essential to win the child's confidence. A number of points need to be considered here.

Nearly all children respond to a warm empathic therapist who shows a positive regard for the child, and listens to and accepts without criticism what the child has to say. When children are shy, resistant or negativistic, a useful technique is to help them associate the therapist with positive feelings from within the child's own experience. Every child has good times that are stored in memory as pictures, sounds and feelings. Encouraging the child to remember the pictures and sounds brings back some of the associated feelings.

These memories are most powerful when thought of exactly as laid down, i.e. recalled from the perspective from which they were originally seen, rather than remembered in a modified form. The therapist can help the child to achieve this through facilitative questions and guesses. A place or event that is likely to be associated with pleasant memories, for example the child's room at home or a recent birthday party, is selected and questions or guesses are then formulated to encourage a vivid recall of the associated pictures and sounds, as in the following example.

'You are at your birthday party sitting at the table waiting for the cake, or is the cake already in front of you? Now who is sitting on your right?' (This is best asked while seated beside the child, facing the same direction and pointing to the right.) 'And who is on your left?' Continue asking about the room, people and food until the child's facial expression is much happier. Then ask the child to remember another time when he was happy and having a good time just like at the birthday party, and elicit a re-creation of that scene. Continue in this way until the child feels more cheerful or is at least as relaxed as the situation will allow. By creating good feelings or being one who makes the child feel good, the therapist becomes a positive figure to the child, and a basis for good rapport has been established.

This can and should be consolidated by identifying and accepting the child's feelings. Children are readily reassured by an adult who warmly and uncritically acknowledges such painful emotions as sadness, guilt, fear and anger. Initial discussion of a child's feelings may, if necessary, be undertaken indirectly, using a variety of techniques.

First, the therapist may say 'I don't know you very well but I've talked to lots of boys and girls in your situation and they told me how sad/angry/worried they were.' Such a statement puts into words how a child feels and offers permission to talk about it.

Second, feelings may be introduced into the conversation by the use of idiom. For example, a therapist energetically told a hospitalized child (afraid of dying but unable to discuss it) of a frightening motoring experience that had 'scared him to death'. After a few moments of thought the child broached the subject of death with his parents. His mother completed the therapeutic sequence by acknowledging his feelings and assuring him that they were understandable and reasonable.

Third, emotions can be brought into the conversation metaphorically by the use of allegorical stories or anecdotes. For example, an angry 16-year-old, who was refusing to cooperate with a very intrusive medical treatment procedure, was told this anecdote:

> Mark, as you were talking about your home it reminded me of mine and for some reason I thought of all the apple trees I have in my backyard. Several years ago when the trees were young and seemingly healthy, we were visited by a friend who grew apples for a living. He noticed that the new apple trees were already sick. He told me that I would have to spray them with several different medications every other week, all summer long, every summer, whether they looked well or sick. At first I was overwhelmed and discouraged but after some thought I decided to do as I had been advised. I had to use one spray to stop bacterial infections, another for fungal infections, a third spray for insects, and a fourth spray for mites. That's a lot of medicine but apparently even normal apple trees need them if they are going to grow and produce apples. Well, I have sprayed them every year for eighteen years and they have grown to be big trees. Every summer these big strong apple trees produce many apples that I eat and share with friends. And, of course, I continue to spray my trees and take care of them.

Use of metaphor to explore emotions is discussed further elsewhere (Fosson and Quan, 1984).

Whatever technique is used for discussion of feelings, their acknowledgement and acceptance is in itself highly therapeutic (Truax and Carkhuff, 1967) and forms a solid foundation for the establishment of a good therapeutic relationship.

9.4 THERAPEUTIC TECHNIQUES

The techniques used depend on such factors as the child's age, maturity, personality and willingness to participate. In addition the therapist has to feel comfortable with the chosen techniques. Some will prefer to adopt a passive and interpretive role, whilst others may choose to be more active and involved, even to the extent of sitting on the floor and playing.

The indications for the use of each technique are discussed in the relevant section. We start with two techniques suitable for younger children. The recommended age range for each approach can only be approximate as levels of maturity vary enormously, and are certainly not exclusively determined by age.

9.4.1 Play therapy

This approach uses play both as a medium for communication and as a metaphor for the child's experiences and reactions. It may be a component of formal psychotherapy (section 9.4.8) or may be used as a technique in its own right. The therapist provides time, space and attention, plus an array of toys such as a family of dolls, cars and trucks, building bricks, animals, fences, modelling material such as playdough, and crayons and paper. Within broad limits the child is allowed to use the toys as desired, and to incorporate the therapist in the play. The child' s attitude towards the therapist and the latter's reaction to the child are noted, as well as the themes of the child's play. The play itself allows the child to gain a sense of control over previous unpleasant experiences to 'get it off his chest' (Bettelheim, 1987). In addition some therapists play with the children and assist them in exploring alternative conceptualizations or actions.

In the former (passive) style the therapist would watch as an abused child placed the infant doll in a block building, constructed for the purpose, and then push a car at the building until it collapsed and the baby was knocked over. In the latter (active) style, the therapist would: (1) talk to the child about how the one in charge of the car must feel good because he is in control, and certainly feels much better than the baby who is being struck by the car; (2) assist the child in making the building (safe place) stronger; and (3) talk about how bad the baby must feel being hit over and over again.

Jane, aged 5, was referred because of her failure to grow and refusal to eat. She played a game with the family doll figures in which the daddy shouted at the mummy, and then went out to work. The mummy then shouted at and smacked the baby, who pushed her dinner away. The therapist linked the baby's distress at seeing her parents argue to the expression of distress by refusing to eat.

Play therapy is of most use in children up to about 10 years old, and is indicated in any situation when such children are being seen individually. It is of particular value in helping children work through (make sense of and express feelings about) traumatic experiences or prepare for feared future events, such as frightening procedures or operations.

9.4.2 Drawing and painting techniques

These are most applicable to children from about 6 years to adolescence. Drawing can provide information on the function of the child as well as providing a useful channel for therapeutic communications. Completely unstructured drawing can be part of every consultation. A low table with pencils and unlined paper is provided and the child is encouraged to draw.

A slightly more structured approach is the squiggle game (Winnicott, 1971). The child is told there are no rules and is invited to add something to an impulsive line drawing (squiggle) made by the therapist. The child then makes a squiggle for the therapist to turn into something. The squiggles are used as a mode of communication. Alternatively the child is asked to draw something specific such as their house or family, the result being used as a focus for discussion.

The treatment starts when the therapist checks out his understanding of the child's communication and proposes some responses or coping strategies. For example, the child in Figure 9.1 started with an arc squiggle and produced a large and small animal. This discordance suggested an unequal relationship, with the small animal a dependant or victim, and the large animal a protector or persecutor. In this case the child confirmed the persecutor/victim interpretation, and the therapist began talking about ways the fish could be protected. The child joined in with his own ideas for protecting the fish, including escape, and proceeded to draw in some of the early suggestions for protection. Ultimately the therapist suggested the possibility of other, and benevolent asymmetrical relationships such as mother–baby relationships, and told the child a truncated version of the Boris and Amos story (Steig, 1971). This concerns mice, whales and rescue. The theme is one of catastrophe for the small and innocent, followed by help from a large, powerful stranger, with subsequent recovery by the victim and a final psychological working through of the experience. When children are in the early stages of their own catastrophe, the introduction of helpful strangers and the anticipation of improvement and recovery (often) brings hope and improved mood.

Drawing as a therapeutic technique may be used in the same circumstances as play therapy, and can be combined with play therapy or be part of other techniques such as psychotherapy (see section 9.4.8).

Figure 9.1 Squiggle game

9.4.3 Counselling

Counselling is suitable for slightly older children, from about 8 years upwards. The focus is on helping the child to cope with reality-based problems (in contrast to psychotherapy, which focuses on the child's inner world). The therapist (or counsellor) aims to help the child cope better with whatever stresses have produced the presenting problem.

For example, Sally, aged 9, was having considerable trouble coming to terms with her recent-onset diabetes, with the subsequent dietary restrictions and frequent insulin injections. Initial discussions revealed how helpless and controlled Sally was feeling. The therapist made this statement:

> I think you can be proud of how well you have behaved taking your medicine and all those injections. Some children I have known have worried that they might run out of blood, or get hurt badly by having blood drawn so many times (identification of feelings). I would be worried too (confirming and accepting their feelings), and a little angry. One boy told me he would like to give his doctor twenty injections so he could see how bad it was (possible fantasy action). You know that it is your body and that you are supposed to be in control of it aren't you? Well maybe you can't stop those injections, but you *can* pick out what you eat or wear, and tell them how angry you are (gaining some control of the situation). In fact you might want to talk to the doctor about just drawing blood every other day or get your mother to talk to him about it.

All this explicit discussion might be followed with an anecdote or metaphor (discussed subsequently) to further illustrate how a 9-year-old might regain some control. Such an approach depends on Sally's continued interest and acceptance. If these are lacking other less direct methods can be tried, such as the use of metaphors or action techniques.

9.4.4 Metaphors

Metaphors are of value when a child resists a direct approach to a problem but can make use of stories or anecdotes. They allow for a continuing dialogue, without disrupting the relationship or triggering embarrassment or other forms of distress. The metaphor conveys an idea in an indirect, yet paradoxically more meaningful way, to which the child can intuitively relate (Mills and Crowley, 1986).

The following example illustrates useful types of metaphorical approaches to communication with children: (1) displacement; for example, the child may be able to discuss the death or loss of his dog or another pet, but not his grandmother; (2) idiom; for example, an anatomical discussion of the nerves carrying messages of pain from the abdomen may trigger a discussion of 'nerves' or anxiety as the cause of an illness; (3) story theme; for example, the story of the three little pigs and the big bad wolf (persecutor/victim theme) is useful in discussions and dramatic play with physically and sexually abused children; (4) drawing; for example, 'a monster tree in the side yard that might fall on your home' was the picture produced during the squiggle game (see section 9.4.2) by a boy who had been sexually molested by an adolescent neighbour; (e) board games, for example snakes and ladders (a children's game of repeated advances and setbacks) has special meaning and interest to youngsters with chronic relapsing illnesses, whilst cartoons, for example the Road Runner or Danger-mouse, communicate invincibility to children feeling particularly vulnerable. Mills and Crowley (1986) have provided an excellent text on therapeutic metaphors for children.

9.4.5 Action techniques

These include role play, social skills training, sculpting and psychodrama. The common thread to these methods is the exploration of material through postures, fantasizing or acting by child and therapist. As in play therapy, the child can be the director and gain a sense of control as well as providing diagnostic material. Alternatively the therapist can be the director and provide a therapeutic message to the child.

Role play involves pretending with the child; for example, when a child tells of rejection by her deceased mother with great emotion, the therapist might say 'Maybe your mother was thinking: [with feeling] "Oh Mary, I so wanted to protect you from hurt, and I thought that it would help you to start getting used to me not being around, so that it would be easier for you later. I love you so much and want to protect you even when I'll no longer be here." '

Alternatively the child and the therapist could role play a situation which the child finds too difficult to cope with. For example, Hannah, aged 12, admitted to hospital with anorexia nervosa, was very upset by her parents' tendency to play down her distress. Whenever she tried to express painful feelings they minimized or dismissed them. Her therapist used role play to help her find ways of asserting herself and confronting her parents.

Social skills training also involves role play and focuses on helping children to cope with social situations that they are likely to find difficult. The emphasis is on being prepared by anticipating problems, developing a plan of action, and practising the implementation of that plan.

For example, an adolescent who deliberately took an excessive number of her mother's sedatives is being discharged from the hospital and anticipating a return to school in two days. She is asked how she will respond to the inevitable question, 'What happened?' She is assisted with the answer until it is honest, protects her privacy, and affords her comfort. Finally the therapist, in the role of a peer, poses the question in various situations and ways, until the patient feels that she can handle the question without being overwhelmed.

Social skills training can also be carried out with advantage in a group setting, each member taking a different role.

Sculpting is also a pretend game, with the child placing and posturing the therapist to simulate an important person (e.g., a parent or teacher) as experienced in their day-to-day life. The child plays himself and each member comments about their feelings in the positions. Next the child places and positions the members of the dyad as he wants them to be, and/or as they 'should be'. The differences are discussed and the reasonableness of the child's desires are confirmed. The technique allows exploration and practice of alternatives.

Psychodrama utilizes similar principles, with a skit, mime or some other scenario being acted during the session.

Ben, aged 9, had been referred because of recurrent headaches. He was of modest intelligence and at school was failing to fulfil his parents' expectations. The therapist suggested that he and Ben play a game of mimes and each guess what the other's represented. The therapist had learned that Ben's family had not acknowledged his limited achievements on the piano. One of the therapist's mimes that Ben later repeated over and over was a concert pianist who played very seriously, and then smiled broadly, while bowing repeatedly and slowly beginning to look very proud. It was as if Ben was beginning to learn to value his own achievements. Certainly his headaches diminished and eventually ceased.

9.4.6 Cognitive therapy

This focuses on helping the child to learn adaptive strategies to solve various problems. For example, children can be taught not to make immediate and maladaptive responses, but rather to think through their options and make decisions about the best course of action.

Janice, aged 10, had a severe metabolic disorder necessitating tiresome dietary restrictions. Whenever she had an argument with her brother she would break the diet. She was taught to consider the consequences of this, and helped to draw up a list of alternative responses. Further discussion assisted her in deciding upon the best response—leaving the room. The use of cognitive therapy for children has been described in detail by Kendall (1981).

9.4.7 Relaxation techniques

These include muscle relaxation, biofeedback and hypnotherapy, and are applicable for children of 5 years and upwards (Gardner and Olness, 1981). They work by helping children to gain control over muscle tension. *Muscle relaxation* is learned by concentrating on the tension in various muscle groups, and alternately contracting and relaxing them (a programme specifically designed for children has been prepared by Ollendick and Cerny, 1983). *Biofeedback* uses machinery to provide information on pulse rate, skin humidity or blood pressure, so that the child can learn to modify these physiological measures by self-relaxation. *Hypnotherapy* utilizes the induction of a state of altered consciousness to elicit deep relaxation. A number of different strategies are available to induce hypnosis (Gardner and Olness, 1981) and can be used for children aged 7 years and upwards.

Examples of useful inductions include: (1) having young children close their eyes and imagine their favourite place; and (2) teaching adolescents muscle relaxation, and then suggesting that they might like to close their eyes and imagine a pleasant situation. The therapist, using a calm and mellow voice, weaves the words 'comfort' and 'relaxation' into the conversation, timing these to coincide with the child breathing out.

These techniques seem to be of value for anxiety-related disorders of whatever nature, and for the relief of physical symptoms such as pain and itching, as well as for preparing children for unpleasant or frightening medical and surgical procedures. Painful or otherwise distressing sensations can be blocked by teaching the child to imagine them as if they were like an electric circuit such as a light switch. The child then learns to 'switch on and off' the unpleasant sensation.

9.4.8 Psychotherapy

The essence of child psychotherapy is the use of the relationship between the therapist and the child to help resolve the child's problems. The medium for communication might be any combination of talking, drawing and play to help the understanding and expression of unconscious material. The theories underlying its practice are complex but have been comprehensively reviewed by Smirnoff (1971), amongst others. The most influential theorists and practitioners have been Anna Freud (e.g., 1966), Melanie Klein (e.g., 1948) and Donald Winnicott (e.g., 1971).

Careful attention is paid to using an appropriate setting where the child feels safe and comfortable, and in which there is suitable 'play' material. Privacy should be ensured, and the same time each week should be allocated for the particular child. In this way a therapeutic alliance is developed in which the therapist helps the child to explore and understand areas of confusion and concern.

Rachel was referred for psychotherapy at the age of 9, following her parents' separation. For four years she had suffered recurrent abdominal pain and episodes of vomiting for which no organic cause could be found. Rachel saw her father for alternate weekends, and her future stepfather visited the family frequently, although he did not stay overnight. She was very quiet in the presence of either man.

Rachel was seen at weekly intervals by a male therapist to whom she initially related in a very shy manner. As she gained confidence she involved him in play, and produced several drawings, all of which emphasized men as bad. When the therapist compared her increasing enjoyment of the sessions with her feelings about men, she would immediately become quiet and complain of stomachache. As the therapist gently persisted with this theme, Rachel gradually became more angry towards him and eventually would tear up her pictures and throw toys at him. He contained and accepted her anger and interpreted it as an expression of her feeling towards her father and future stepfather. Over the succeeding weeks she started talking about her feelings of being disliked and rejected by her father, and her anger towards her stepfather. As she became more able to express directly these negative feelings so her physical symptoms ceased.

Child psychotherapy is indicated for deeply entrenched problems which are not amenable to family therapy, or when it is not possible to involve the family in therapy. The child must be able (1) to distinguish between fantasy and reality, (2) to form a relationship with another person, and (3) to recognize and verbalize thoughts and feelings. The parents or guardians must be prepared to support the therapy.

Psychoanalysis is a far more intensive form of psychotherapy, usually including the use of the famous 'couch', and being offered on a five times a week basis. There has never been any satisfactory evidence that the additional intensity and expense is of any value in any disorder.

The following case example illustrates the points made in this chapter and summarizes the applicability of individual therapies in childhood illness.

9.5 CASE ILLUSTRATION

A 14-year-old girl with chronic renal disease was first seen the day before a nephrectomy. She was a sallow, frail, slight, sad child lying in her hospital bed, surrounded by gaily coloured posters, get-well cards and stuffed animals. As she talked her hands were busily cutting, folding and rolling paper flowers intended as gifts for the surgeons of the next morning. Mother and daughter were quiet and distracted as they related the story of their heart-breaking summer.

Mother had given her kidney to Jessica three months earlier in a second desperate attempt to save her daughter's life. A summer of medical reversals had shaken mother's confidence and brought suspicions of surgical misadventures. The impending removal of the rejected kidney had now finally brought feelings of complete defeat. Mother did not wish to be directly involved in any counselling sessions and other members of the family were not available, so individual therapy was undertaken.

Early on, rapport was established by asking Jessica to describe her home and the good times that she had experienced before her parents' divorce. Without the communicative skills or permission to off-load she had become increasingly depressed, had lost her appetite and had abandoned any hope. Although she professed affection and admiration for the doctors and surgeons, anger flashed across her face when the therapist gave voice to her feelings. He accepted her anger and defence as appropriate and reasonable under the circumstances.

During the next month, the following actions were taken or encouraged. The physicians and nurses were prepared for the patient to become assertive. The mother said that it was all right with her if Jessica 'told people what she thought' even though she (mother) did not. Explicit instructions were given in the first person: 'When I think someone is doing me wrong I tell them how I feel about it, why I feel that way, and how I want things to change.' When a social worker was upset with the therapist, the conversation was moved a few steps to Jessica's room. Thus Jessica was exposed to modelling of assertiveness and resolution as the social worker expressed her feelings, and the therapist and social worker gradually resolved their differences. Jessica had seen assertiveness in action without it harming anyone, and with some gain for the initiator. Anecdotes or stories of assertive and dependent children and animals were also related.

As recovery from surgery progressed, and Jessica stabilized on dialysis, she was placed in a regular physical activity group for depressed hospitalized children. During this period, Jessica began feeling better and concurrently became more active, happier and more assertive. Finally one day when she had been promised weekend leave, the resident physician reneged because Jessica had fallen and sprained her ankle. She became very angry, sought out the chief paediatrician and informed him of how she felt, why she felt that way and insisted that she should have her weekend leave. Of course this was granted, and this reward, plus praise from the therapist and nurses, reinforced Jessica's assertiveness, which eventually became a permanent part of her personality, and enabled her to cope with numerous medical complications.

9.6 SUMMARY

Individual therapies are wide-ranging in their style and usefulness. They can be used separately and in combination, and may be complementary to other therapies. They offer a powerful method of assisting children to adjust and cope, but can be expensive and time-consuming. They can be used as an only treatment for a child, but are more commonly and productively incorporated into a comprehensive management plan. The effective therapist (1) is aware of the themes which are concealed beneath the surface of the child's messages, (2) has an armamentarium of basic therapeutic concepts, and (3) is able to implement a communication strategy or treatment method in which these concepts can be effectively transmitted.

CHAPTER 10

Pharmacotherapy

The therapy happens not in the patient, nor in the doctor but between the two of them (Balint, 1973)

GUIDE FOR THE READER

Balint's advice is an important reminder that it is how we relate to our clients that matters just as much, if not more, than any drugs we prescribe. With that proviso we offer in this chapter a brief review of available medication when somatization is involved. We hope that it will be of value for medically trained readers, and informative and interesting to those who are not handicapped by the wish to wave a pharmacological wand.

10.1 INTRODUCTION

There is an understandable tendency to seek a safe and simple solution when managing somatization disorders. Unfortunately the use of pharmacological agents is rarely safe, simple or the solution. For these reasons, the following principles should be applied:

(1) Medication should be prescribed only after a detailed assessment of the situation, which ideally includes a family interview and a school report.
(2) There should always be a clearly defined reason for the use of medication, and a specified length of treatment after which the situation should be reviewed.
(3) Medication should never be used in isolation; other aspects of management such as parental counselling should always be included.
(4) Parental consent and cooperation is essential for the successful use of medication; fear of side-effects or addiction, or ambivalence for other reasons may all militate against compliance.

An important but all too often neglected aspect of pharmacotherapy is that of compliance. Non-compliance (failure to take the prescribed medication in the correct dose) occurs in at least one-third of medical patients (Flach, 1988);

greater non-compliance can be expected by patients on long-term or preventive treatment (about 50%), and even more for psychiatric patients where behavioural issues are the primary concern. Less is known about compliance by children and their parents, but nothing can be taken for granted. For instance, results from a study of diabetics showed that even where patients complied with daily urine testing they did not always take the necessary medication (Stuart, 1982). Compliance with pharmacological treatment in a group of hyperactive children varied from 0 to 100%, with a mean of 67% (Kaufman *et al.*, 1981).

The key variables known to affect compliance include the patient, doctor–patient relationship, the actual treatment regime and the patient's family (Flach, 1988). In childhood the attitudes of the family are of particular relevance. Fear of or actual side effects, frequency of drug administration, complexity of the regimen, lack of clarity in the instructions and prolonged periods of treatment all conspire to reduce compliance. The physician needs to assess parental attitudes to treatment, to acknowledge any concerns, and to allay anxieties by patient exploration and explanation. Parents should be given as full an explanation as possible of the purpose of the medication, the length of time for which it should be used, possible side effects, and the action to be taken if side effects should occur. This apparently time-consuming procedure is a vital insurance against the high risk of non-compliance. A positive parental attitude is far more likely to produce satisfactory compliance than ambivalence or uncertainty.

Once treatment has commenced, continuing discussions with the parents are indicated. The frequency of side effects, occasional behavioural changes, and latent fears such as the possibility of impairing school performance or even development, all need to be discussed as a means of allaying parental anxiety. It is often important to ensure that school staff are aware of the need for medication (if taken during school time), and of possible side effects such as impaired concentration or drowsiness.

At the same time as placing such emphasis on the medication, it is equally important to stress to parents that medication is only part of the treatment. How the parents manage the problem requires continuing attention, and other treatments such as family or individual therapy may well be necessary. It requires a fine balancing act to maintain sufficient attention to (possibly several) contrasting approaches.

In the following section we have listed those groups of medications that might be used in somatization disorders, but in each instance their use should be complementary to other forms of treatment.

10.2 ANALGESICS

These are of value only for the immediate treatment of pain, and remain useful only if they are used infrequently. They should not be used on a regular basis.

Aspirin should not be used at all in childhood because of the rare but serious danger of Reye's syndrome.

Paracetamol is readily available but should be used judiciously and not exceeding 500 mg 4–6-hourly. Far better though to understand and overcome the underlying problem.

10.3 ANTIEMETICS

These are of value for the symptomatic treatment of nausea and vomiting in 'periodic syndrome' and 'cyclical vomiting'. There are numerous preparations available, including hyoscine and various antihistamines such as cyclizine and chlorpheniramine. They all have such side effects as drowsiness, dry mouth and blurred vision. Dosage, as with all medication in childhood, is weight-dependent, and should start low. The range is as follows: hyoscine 75–300 μg four times daily; cyclizine 25 mg three times daily. In intractable cases of cyclical vomiting a phenothiazine such as chlorpromazine should be used, if necessary intramuscularly, up to 50 mg three times daily (see phenothiazines).

10.4 ANTIMIGRAINE AGENTS

When the diagnosis of migraine is truly established, medication is of considerable value. The acute attack can be treated with paracetamol, preferably in dispersible or effervescent form, as absorption may be impaired by reduced peristalsis. Dosage should be in the order of 250–500 mg 4–6-hourly. Antiemetics may also help.

When attacks occur more than once a month a short prophylactic course may be tried. Clonidine (see section 10.12) 25–50 μg twice daily, and propranolol (see section 10.11) 20 mg two to three times daily, are both helpful in 60–70% of cases.

10.5 ANTISPASMODICS

This range of drugs is of limited value but can be tried in 'cyclical vomiting' and 'periodic syndrome' as they act by reducing intestinal spasm. Dicyclomine, 10–20 mg three times daily, is amongst those most commonly prescribed in childhood. Although its value and safety in infantile (three-month) colic has been hotly disputed, Illingworth (1987), amongst others, recommends its use for such infants in a dose of 5 mg up to three to four times daily before feeds.

10.6 LAXATIVES

Whilst the use of laxatives as a routine in children is undesirable, they are usually essential in constipation, especially when overflow occurs. Although mild constipation may be remedied by increasing dietary fibre or fruit juice intake, in most instances laxatives, singly or in combination, will be necessary.

10.6.1 Bulk-forming

Bran in any form increases faecal mass and stimulates peristalsis after a few days, so can be used in mild types of constipation, but not where there is faecal impaction or overflow. Methylcellulose and ispaghula husk are bulk-forming agents available in various proprietary forms.

10.6.2 Stimulants

These act by increasing peristalsis about 8–12 hours after ingestion. Senna in its myriad forms is the best known and should be given in half the adult dose.

10.6.3 Softeners

These act by lubricating or softening the faeces, and are available in the form of liquid paraffin or dioctyl sodium sulphosuccinate. They should be administered in a third to a half of the adult dose.

10.6.4 Suppositories and enemas

These should be reserved for resistant cases. They work by lubricating and softening impacted faeces, with consequent bowel movements. Suppositories should be tried first and are usually available as a paediatric preparation. Enemas should be administered in half the adult dose.

10.7 ANTIDIARRHOEAL PREPARATIONS

For chronic non-specific diarrhoea, but not infective diarrhoea, loperamide is relatively safe in a dose of 1–4 mg up to four times daily. Providing the child is thriving treatment should not be prolonged.

10.8 PHARMACOLOGICAL TREATMENT OF ENURESIS

The only pharamacological agents of proven value within the hierarchy of treatment for enuresis are the tricyclic antidepressants, for example imipramine and amitriptyline (see section 10.14). Their mode of action in enuresis is not understood, for none of the known effects of tricyclics (antidepressant activity, alteration of sleep rhythm, anticholinergic and antiadrenergic activity) have been shown to be a key factor in their effectiveness (Shaffer and Ambrosini, 1985). Dosage is in the order of 25–50 mg at bedtime. They usually prevent bed-wetting, but relapse on cessation of medication is common if other behavioural treatments are not incorporated.

10.9 ANTICONVULSANTS

The wide range of drugs in this group is beyond the scope of this book. They should only be used when there is clear evidence (clinical or EEG) of seizure activity. The commonly used anticonvulsants such as phenobarbitone, phenytoin, primidone, carbamazepine, ethosuximide, sulthiame and sodium valproate can all have potentially troublesome side effects, including drowsiness, sedation, depression, irritability, distractibility and learning problems. Carbamazepine is also of value in children who suffer marked mood swings and may be used as an alternative to lithium.

10.10 HYPNOTICS AND SEDATIVES

Sleep disorders may occur in isolation, or be secondary to other problems such as anxiety, depression or physical illness. Isolated sleep disorders should be treated behaviourally, but if this fails a number of different drugs are available, all of which are relatively safe. The mildest agents are chloral (30–50 mg/kg, up to a maximum single dose of 1 g), promethazine and trimeprazine (10–100 mg in a single dose one hour before bedtime). Stronger drugs include nitrazepam (2.5–5 mg) and dichloralphenazone (450–900 mg) but these should be reserved for older children with severe sleep disturbance. Night terrors can be treated with diazepam (see below).

Each of these medications causes drowsiness and frequently the next morning the child might experience headache, irritability or a hangover effect. In larger doses they can be used as sedatives for intense anxiety or preoperative preparation. None should be used for more than 2–3 weeks, to avoid dependence.

10.11 MINOR TRANQUILLIZERS

This range of drugs, sometimes known as anxiolytics, are of limited use for children. Where high levels of anxiety underlie or accompany a physical disorder a short course may be of some value. When the child is expressing overt anxiety (i.e. a subjective experience of morbid anticipation) lorazepam (1–2 mg daily in divided doses) or diazepam (1–5 mg daily in divided doses) can be tried. If the anxiety is expressed more physiologically (i.e. sweating, palpitations, abdominal discomfort or pain, tremor, headaches, nausea or vomiting) a beta-blocker such as propranolol should be considered, in the range of 20–80 mg daily in divided doses. Propranolol is also of value in the treatment of migraine.

Diazepam (5 mg at night) is sometimes helpful in the management of night terrors and sleep-walking, although as with many other disorders behavioural treatments aimed at altering the sleep pattern should be tried first (Lask, 1988d).

10.12 MAJOR TRANQUILLIZERS

Sometimes known as neuroleptics, this range of drugs is of value in a number of different disorders, including extreme agitation, severe and uncontrollable aggression, the psychoses, and movement disorders such as tics and hyperkinesis (Chapter 3). Only the management of the movement disorders is within the scope of this book, although the principles of neuroleptic use are the same whatever the condition. They are powerful drugs which often produce a dramatic relief of symptoms, but at the cost of a wide range of side effects. The most common of these are drowsiness, postural hypotension, dry mouth, constipation, blurred vision and extrapyramidal signs such as rigidity, tremor, restlessness, excess salivation and muscle spasms.

The most well-known neuroleptics, chlorpromazine and haloperidol, should be reserved for the treatment of major psychiatric disorders such as psychosis, uncontrolled aggression and extreme agitation. They may also be used in the management of tics and hyperkinesis, but the frequency of side effects dictates that they should only be used for these conditions when other medication fails. The starting dose for haloperidol is 0.025 mg/kg daily in divided doses, increasing gradually until a therapeutic effect is achieved, but not exceeding 0.1 mg/kg daily. Chlorpromazine should be initiated at 25–50 mg daily in divided doses, increasing to 300 mg daily maximum. If extrapyramidal side effects occur, treatment should ideally be stopped, but if there is no alternative, antiparkinsonian agents such as orphenadrine 100–200 mg daily, or benzhexol 4–8 mg daily, in divided doses should be introduced.

Tics are best treated with clonidine 25 μg, two to three times daily, or pimoside 1–2 mg daily in one or two doses. Trifluperidol has a similar action to haloperidol but it is said to have fewer side effects, and might therefore be tried in a dose of 250 μg to 2 mg daily, if clonidine or pimoside fails.

10.13 STIMULANTS

The main stimulants are methylphenidate and dexamphetamine, although the latter has fallen into considerable disrepute because of the dangers of abuse, addiction and psychosis. The only indications for the use of stimulants are (1) hyperkinesis (Chapter 3), and (2) narcolepsy (very rare and beyond the scope of this book).

Methylphenidate is the drug of choice in hyperkinesis and is usually given at breakfast and lunchtime, starting at 0.3 mg/kg daily and slowly increasing to 1.0 mg/kg daily. It is customary to omit medication at the weekends when, theoretically, symptom control is less essential, to reduce the side effects such as loss of appetite, sleep disturbance and, in the long term, growth delay. The apparent paradox of using a stimulant for a condition manifested by hyperactivity is explained by its action of stimulating the reticular *inhibitory* centre, thus producing a slowing down effect.

10.14 ANTIDEPRESSANTS

As with so many other psychotropic drugs, antidepressants have a limited role in childhood disorders. Their use should be restricted to the treatment of enuresis (see section 3.5.1) and in true depressive disorder, as manifested by psychomotor retardation with mood, sleep and appetite disturbance (Lask, 1988a). The only antidepressants that should be used in children are the tricyclics. Monoamine oxidase inhibitors (MAOIs) have potentially disastrous side effects if dietary restrictions are not adhered to and, given the absence of any evidence for their superiority over tricyclics, they should not be used.

Where depression does exist, whether or not it is disguised by physical symptoms, amitriptyline or imipramine may be used, in one dose of 25–150 mg at night. The side effects of dry mouth, dizziness, blurred vision and constipation occur with both drugs but tend to be less marked with amitriptyline. The therapeutic effect does not occur for 10–14 days after starting treatment, although with enuresis symptomatic relief usually occurs much sooner.

Clomipramine, another tricyclic, is said to be of particular value when depression is accompanied by obsessional behaviour. It can be given as one dose, 25–75 mg, at night.

10.15 LITHIUM

This drug is of most value in those very rare instances of 'mixed (or bipolar) affective disorder' in which both depression and elation occur, either separately or in combination. There have been claims for its effectiveness in aggressive children with mood disturbance, and in intractable depression.

Monitoring of blood levels is indicated to ensure that the therapeutic range (0.6–1.2 mmol/l) is maintained. Initially this should be done weekly, but once levels are stable monthly checks are sufficient. Lower levels are ineffective and higher levels produce such side effects as gastrointestinal disturbances, tremor, blurred vision, polyuria and polydipsia.

10.16 SUMMARY

Pharmacological treatments are not the panacea we might wish, but used judiciously they make an important contribution in the management of the disorders discussed in this book. Medication should always be used in complement with other forms of treatment, and careful explanation and discussion is necessary to ensure compliance. Side effects are common and treatment should therefore be time-limited whenever possible.

Epilogue

During the course of one clinic six very different children were seen for the first time. Tony, 14, had very poorly controlled asthma necessitating frequent hospital admissions; Alice, 13, was suffering from persistent and frequent diarrhoea for which no organic cause could be found; Adam, 11, had recurrent sore throats and fever, and in consequence was missing a considerable amount of school; Stuart, 9, had frequent and overwhelming headaches; Rama, 7, was curled up like a ball, without speaking or moving; and Danya, 5, who had recently been treated for pellagra (a form of vitamin deficiency) complained of severe pains in her feet and hands. The children spanned the age range, came from different cultures, and social backgrounds, and their presenting problems had very little in common. Each had been fully investigated elsewhere and no obvious cause found for the unremitting nature of their symptoms.

Tony was the eldest of three children of totally deaf parents, and from early in life had acted as interpreter for his parents, using sign language and lip reading. When his asthma developed at the age of four, his parents had to devise special means of ensuring his safety at night, as they couldn't hear him coughing or wheezing. It proved difficult for them to relinquish their highly protective role. As he entered his teens he became increasingly irritated by their involvement and inability to let go which contrasted so markedly with their dependence on him as an interpreter. He was unable to discuss these feelings for fear of upsetting his parents, with subsequent and frequent exacerbations of asthma. One session of family therapy was sufficient to help Tony to explain to his parents how he felt and to work out ways of demonstrating to them that he was capable of looking after himself. His two younger sisters were given more responsibility for interpreting to their parents, who in turn were complimented on having coped so well with their disability. They were also advised of Tony's need to learn how to cope alone, as it would not be long before he would be leaving home.

Alice's diarrhoea started after a holiday abroad, during which the whole family had suffered from gastroenteritis, and the parents' long-standing conflict had been exacerbated. Her illness did seem to unite the parents in their concern, and to postpone any decision about separation. A recommendation for marital therapy was cautiously accepted and once Alice's parents began to tackle their differences her symptoms gradually resolved.

Adam's throat infections commenced at the time he transferred to a high-achieving school, and this coincided with his father being told that he was suffering from 'post-viral fatigue syndrome'. It was assumed by the family and several doctors that Adam had the same condition, and accordingly he was treated as if he had a chronic illness. Adam also had been diagnosed some years previously as having 'dyslexia', although his reading skills were now almost par for age. He just about managed to keep up with his school-work but tended to score lower than average, and was frequently criticized by his teachers. A clear statement to Adam and his parents about the true cause of his symptoms and transfer to a less demanding and more sympathetic school led to a rapid improvement.

Despite intensive physical investigation no cause had been found for Stuart's headaches, which had started shortly after his recovery from a viral encephalopathy. Following his parents' divorce his mother had remarried and one year later had given birth to twins. His stepfather was very preoccupied with his job, and his mother spent most of her time with the twins. He saw his own father on alternate weekends. There could be little doubt that Stuart's headaches were an expression of his distress and loneliness. A short course of individual therapy helped him to express his despair and to talk openly about it in the family. Although it proved difficult to change the family situation, his headaches resolved.

Rama had stopped talking several weeks previously, and in the last few days had also stopped eating. She was now no longer doing anything for herself and was totally immobile. It took many months of intensive nursing care and patient building of trust, before she was well enough to reveal that for the six months prior to hospital admission her uncle had been sexually abusing her.

Danya had an obscure metabolic disorder causing her to develop a vitamin deficiency disorder, pellagra, which manifested itself by skin rashes, diarrhoea, tearfulness, and numbness in her fingers and toes. Appropriate treatment reversed the deficiency with gradual resolution of all her symptoms, except for her tears. At the time for discharge from hospital she started complaining of pain at the sites where previously there had been numbness. No physical cause could be found but further questioning revealed that she had been the butt of considerable teasing at school because of her skin rashes, and she was frightened of returning. Relaxation treatment combined with gentle encouragement to make gradual contact with school friends and teachers helped her to return to school, after which her remaining symptoms resolved.

Despite the considerable differences between each child, there were many factors in common. In each case there were physical symptoms the nature and/ or intensity of which could not be explained in purely organic terms. Although not always immediately obvious there were in each instance clear-cut predisposing, precipitating, and perpetuating factors. Once these had been taken into account and appropriate treatment instituted, the symptoms resolved. Truly the children were talking with their bodies.

References

Ables, B. S., and Brandsma, J. M. (1977) *Therapy for Couples.* Jossey-Bass, San Francisco.

Alexander, F. (1950). *Psychosomatic Medicine.* Norton, New York.

American Psychiatric Association (1980) *Diagnostic and Statistical Manual of Mental Disorders* (3rd edn) (DSM-III). American Psychiatric Association, Washington, DC.

American Psychiatric Association (1987) *Diagnostic and Statistical Manual of Mental Disorders* (3rd edn), revised (DSM-IIIR). American Psychiatric Association, Washington, DC.

Anderson, C. M., and Stewart, S. (1983) *Mastering Resistance: A Practical Guide to Family Therapy.* Guilford Press, New York.

Apley, J. (1963) Family patterning and childhood disorders. *Lancet*, i, 67.

Apley, J. (1971) Mass media and the child. *Proceedings of the Royal Society of Medicine*, **64**, 341–342.

Apley, J. (1982) One child. In: J. Apley and C. Ounsted (eds), *One Child.* Spastics International Medical Publications, London.

Apley, J., McKeith, R., and Meadow, R. (1978) *The Child and His Symptoms: A Comprehensive Approach* (3rd edn). Blackwell, Oxford.

Baker, G. (1987) Psychological factors and immunity. *Journal of Psychosomatic Research*, **31**, 1–10.

Balint, M. (1973) Research in psychotherapy. In: E. Balint and J. S. Norell (eds), *Six Minutes for the Patient: Interactions in General Practice Consultation.* Tavistock, London.

Bandura, A. (1974) *Social Learning Theory.* Prentice-Hall, Englewood Cliffs, New Jersey.

Bannister, D., and Fransella, F. (1971) *Inquiring Man: The Theory of Personal Constructs.* Penguin, Harmondsworth.

Barker, P. (1985) *Using Metaphors in Psychotherapy.* Brunner Mazel, New York.

Barr, R. (1983) Pain tolerance and developmental change. In: M. D. Levine, W. Carey, A. Crocker, and R. Gross (eds), *Pain Perception.* Saunders, Philadelphia.

Barrows, H. (ed.) (1980) The neurologist's clinical reasoning process. In: *Guide to Neurological Assessment.* Lippincott, Philadelphia.

Bentovim, A. (1987) Physical and sexual abuse of children: The role of the family therapist. *Journal of Family Therapy*, **9**, 383–388.

Bentovim, A., Barnes, G. G., and Cooklin, A. (eds) (1987a) *Family Therapy: Complementary Framework of Theory and Practice.* Academic Press, London.

Bentovim, A., Elton, A., Hildebrand, J., Tranter, M., and Vizard, E. (1987b) *Sexual Abuse Within The Family: Assessment and Treatment.* John Wright, Bristol.

Berger, M. (1985) Psychological assessment and testing. In: M. Rutter and L. Hersov (eds), *Child and Adolescent Psychiatry: Modern Approaches.* Blackwell Scientific Publications, Oxford.

Bettelheim, B. (1987) The importance of play. *Atlantic Monthly* (March), 35–46.

144

Bibace, R., and Walsh, M. (1981) *Children's Conceptions of Health, Illness and Bodily Functions*. Jossey-Bass, Washington.

Bingley, L., Leonard, J., Hensman, S., Lask, B., and Wolff, O. (1980) The comprehensive management of children on a paediatric ward: A family approach. *Archives of Disease in Childhood*, 55, 555–561.

Boone, D., and Hartman, B. (1972) The benevolent over-reaction: A well-intentioned but malignant influence on the handicapped child. *Clinical Pediatrics*, 11, 268–271.

Bowlby, J. (1969) *Attachment and Loss. Vol. I: Attachment*. Hogarth Press and Institute of Psycho-Analysis, London; Basic Books, New York.

Bryant-Waugh, R., Knibbs, J., Fosson, A., Kaminski, Z., and Lask, B. (1988) Long-term follow-up of patients with early onset anorexia nervosa. *Archives of Disease in Childhood*, 63, 5–9.

Cadman, D., Boyle, M., Szatmare, P., and Offord, D. (1987) Chronic illness, disability, and mental and social well-being: Findings of the Ontario Child Health Study. *Pediatrics*, 79, 805–813.

Calabrese, J., Kling, M., and Gold, P. (1987) Alterations in immunocompetence during stress, bereavement, and depression: Focus on neuroendocrine regulation. *American Journal of Psychiatry*, 144, 1123–1134.

Cantwell, D., and Baker, L. (1985) Speech and language development and disorders. In: M. Rutter and L. Hersov (eds), *Child and Adolescent Psychiatry: Modern Approaches*. Blackwell Scientific Publications, Oxford.

Chadwick, D., and Usiskin, S. (1987) *Living with Epilepsy*. MacDonald, London.

Cooper, C. (1978) Child abuse and neglect: Medical aspects. In: S. M. Smith (ed.), *The Maltreatment of Children*. MTP Press, Lancaster.

Dindmeyer, D., and Mckay, G. (1982) *Systematic Training for Effective Parenting: Parent's Handbook*. American Guidance Service, Circle Pines, Minnesota.

Dische, S., Yule, W., Corbett, J., and Hand, D. (1983) Childhood nocturnal enuresis: Factors associated with outcome of treatment with an enuretic alarm. *Developmental Medicine and Child Neurology*, 25, 67–80.

Dubowitz, V., and Hersov, L. (1976) Management of children with non-organic (hysterical) disorders of motor function. *Developmental Medicine and Child Neurology*, 18, 358–368.

Duhl, K., Kantor, D., and Duhl, B. (1973) Learning space and action in family therapy. In: D. A. Bloch (ed.), *Techniques of Family Psychotherapy*. Grune & Stratton, New York.

Dungar, D. B., Pritchard, J., Hensman, S., Leonard, J. V., Lask, B., and Wolff, O. (1986) The investigation of atypical psychosomatic illness: A team approach to diagnosis. *Clinical Pediatrics*, 25, 341–344.

Editorial (1985) Emotion and immunity. *Lancet*, ii, 133–134.

Editorial (1987) Depression, stress, and immunity. *Lancet*, i, 1467–1468.

Egger, J., Carter, C. M., Wilson, J., Turner, M. W., and Soothill, J. F. (1983) Is migraine food allergy? A double blind controlled trial of oligoantigenic diet treatment. *Lancet*, ii, 865–869.

Egger, J., Carter, C. M., Graham, P. J., Gumley, D., and Soothill, J. F. (1985) Controlled trial of oligoantigenic treatment in the hyperkinetic syndrome. *Lancet*, i, 540–545.

Engel, G. L. (1968) A reconsideration of the role of conversion in somatic disease. *Comprehensive Psychiatry*, 9, 316–326.

Feingold, B. F. (1975) Hyperkinesis and learning disabilities linked to artificial food flavors and colors. *American Journal of Nursing*, 75, 797–803.

Fenton, T., and Milla, P. (1988) The irritable bowel syndrome. In: J. T. Harries, P. Milla and D. P. Muller (eds), *Harries' Paediatric Gastroenterology*. Churchill Livingstone, Edinburgh.

Ferreira, A. J. (1963) Family myth and homeostasis. *Archives of General Psychiatry*, **9**, 457–463.

Flach, F. F. (1988) *Psychobiology and Psychopharmacology*. Norton, New York.

Ford, C. V. (1986) The somatizing disorders. *Psychosomatics*, **27**, 327–337.

Fosson, A., and Quan, M. (1984) Reassuring and talking with hospitalized children. *Children's Health Care*, **13**, 37–44.

Fosson, A., and Wilson, J. (1987) Family interactions surrounding feeding of infants with nonorganic failure to thrive. *Clinical Paediatrics*, **26**, 518–523.

Fosson, A., Knibbs, J., Bryant-Waugh, R., and Lask, B. (1987) Early onset anorexia nervosa. *Archives of Disease in Childhood*, **62**, 114–118.

Freud, A. (1966) *Normality and Pathology in Childhood: Assessments of Development*. Hogarth Press, London; International Universities Press, New York.

Friedman, M. (1969) *Pathogenesis of Coronary Artery Disease*. McGraw-Hill, New York.

Fritz, G. (1987) Factors in fatal childhood asthma. *American Journal of Orthopsychiatry*, **57**, 253–257.

Frude, N. (1980) Methodological problems in the evaluation of family therapy. *Journal of Family Therapy*, **2**, 29–44.

Gale, A. (1985) On doing research: The dream and the reality. *Journal of Family Therapy*, **7**, 187–211

Gardner, G. G., and Olness, K. (1981) *Hypnosis and Hypnotherapy with Children*. Grune & Stratton, New York.

Garmezy, N. (1984) Stress-resistant children: The search for protective factors. In: J. E. Stevenson (ed.), *Recent Research in Developmental Psychopathology*. Pergamon Press, Oxford; Mosby, St Louis.

Garmezy, N., and Rutter, M. (1985) Acute reaction to stress. In: M. Rutter and L. Hersov (eds), *Child and Adolescent Psychiatry: Modern approaches* (2nd edn). Blackwell, Oxford; Mosby, St Louis.

Goodyer, I., and Taylor, D. (1985) Hysteria. *Archives of Disease in Childhood*, **60**, 680–681.

Gould, S. (1982) *How to Raise a Responsible Child*. St Martin's Press, New York.

Graham, D. (1972) Psychosomatic medicine. In: N. S. Greenfield and R. A. Sternbach (eds), *Handbook of Psychophysiology*. Holt, Rinehart & Winston, New York.

Graham, P. (1986) *Child Psychiatry: A Developmental Approach*. Oxford University Press, Oxford.

Gratton-Smith, P., Fairley, M., and Procopis, P. (1988) Clinical features of conversion disorder. *Archives of Disease in Childhood*, **63**, 408–414.

Graziano, A., De Giovanni, K., and Garcia, K. (1979) Behavioural treatment of children's fears: A review. *Psychological Bulletin*, **86**, 804–830.

Gregg, I. (1983) Epidemiological aspects. In: T. J. H. Clark and S. Godfrey (eds), *Asthma* (2nd edn). Chapman & Hall, London.

Grolnick, L. (1972) A family perspective of psychosomatic factors in illness. *Family Process*, **11**, 451–486.

Gurman, A. S., and Kniskern, D. P. (1981) *Handbook of Family Therapy*. Brunner Mazel, New York.

Haggerty, R. (1982) Life stress, illness and social support. In J. Apley and C. Ounstead (eds), *One Child*. Spastics International Medical Publications, London; Lippincott, Philadelphia.

Hardwick, P. (1989) Families' medical myths. *Journal of Family Therapy*, **11**, 3–27.

Herbert, M. (1987) *Behavioural Treatment of Children with Problems: A Practice Manual*. Academic Press, London.

Hersov, L., and Berg, I. (1980) *Out of School: Modern Perspectives in Truancy and School Refusal.* Wiley, Chichester.

Holmes, T., and Rahe, R. (1967) The Social Readjustment Rating Scale. *Journal of Psychosomatic Research,* **11**, 213–218.

Huang, D. (2600 BC) *Nai-Chung* (first Chinese medical text).

Illingworth, R. S. (1987) *The Normal Child: Some Problems of the Early Years and Their Treatment.* Churchill Livingstone, New York.

Jerrett, W. (1979) Headaches in general practice. *Practitioner,* **222**, 549–555.

Kaufman, R., Smith-Wright, D., Reese, C., Simpson, R., and Jones, F. (1981) Medication compliance in hyperactive children. *Paediatrics and Pharmacology,* **1**, 231–237.

Kendall, P. (1981) Cognitive behavioral interventions with children. In: B. Lahey and A. Kazdin (eds), *Advances in Clinical Child Psychology Vol. 4.* Plenum, New York.

Kirmayer, L. (1986) Somatisation and the social construction of illness experience. In: S. McHugh and T. Vallis (eds), *Illness Behavior: A Multidisciplinary Model.* Plenum: New York.

Klein, M. (1948) *Contributions to Psycho-analysis 1921–1945.* Hogarth Press, London.

Lask, B. (1982a) Psychological treatments in childhood asthma. In: H. B. Valman (ed.), *Recent Advances in Paediatric Therapeutics* (Topics in Paediatrics 3). Pitman, London.

Lask, B. (1982b) The child in the family. In: J. Apley and C. Ounsted (eds), *One Family.* Spastics International Medical Publications, London.

Lask, B. (1985) *Childhood Problems: A Parent's Guide to Tackling Them.* Dunitz, London; Arno, New York.

Lask, B. (1986) The high-achieving child. *Postgraduate Medical Journal,* **62**, 143–145.

Lask, B. (1987a) Editorial: Damned if we do and damned if we don't. *Journal of Family Therapy,* **9**, 381.

Lask, B. (1987b) Physical illness, the family and the setting. In: A. Bentovim, G. G. Barnes and A. Cooklin (eds), *Family Therapy.* Academic Press, London.

Lask, B. (1987c) Family therapy. *British Medical Journal,* **294**, 203–204.

Lask, B. (1988a) Childhood depression. In: P. Williams (ed.), *Depression.* MTP Press, Lancaster.

Lask, B. (1988b) The highly talented child. *Archives of Disease in Childhood,* **63**, 118–119.

Lask, B. (1988c) Psychosocial factors in childhood diabetes and seizure disorders: the family approach. *Paediatrician,* **15**, 95–101.

Lask, B. (1988d) A novel and non-toxic treatment for night terrors. *British Medical Journal,* **297**, 592.

Lask, B. (1989) Family therapy and group therapy. In: G. Burrows, B. Tonge and J. Werry (eds), *Handbook of Child Psychiatry.* Elsevier, Amsterdam.

Lask, B., and Bryant-Waugh, R. (1986) Childhood onset anorexia nervosa. In: R. Meadow (ed.), *Recent Advances in Paediatrics, Vol. 8.* Churchill Livingstone, Edinburgh.

Leigh, H., and Reiser, M. (1980) *The Patient: Biological, Psychological and Social Dimensions of Medical Practice.* Plenum Medical, New York.

Leslie, S. (1988) Diagnosis and treatment of hysterical conversion reactions. *Archives of Disease in Childhood,* **63**, 506–511.

Lidz, T. (1968) Family organization and personality structure. In: N. Bell and E. Vogel (eds), *A Modern Introduction to the Family.* Free Press, New York.

Lieberman, S. (1979) Transgenerational analysis: The geneograms. A technique in family therapy. *Journal of Family Therapy,* **1**, 51–64.

Lipowski, Z. (1967) Review of consultation psychiatry and psychosomatic medicine: II. Clinical aspects. *Psychosomatic Medicine,* **29**, 201–224.

Lipowski, Z. (1974) Physical illness and psychopathology. *International Journal of Psychiatry in Medicine*, 5, 483–497.

Lipowski, Z. (1984) What does the word 'psychosomatic' really mean? A historical and semantic inquiry. *Psychosomatic Medicine*, 46, 153–171.

Lipowski, Z. (1987) Somatization: Medicine's unsolved problem. *Psychosomatics*, 28, 294–297.

Lishman, W. (1987) *Organic Psychiatry: The Psychological Consequences of Cerebral Disorders* (2nd edn). Blackwell Scientific Publications, Oxford.

Lowe, M., and Costello, A. (1976) *Symbolic Play Test*. NFER, Windsor.

Margetts, E. L. (1950) The early history of the word 'psychosomatic'. *Canadian Medical Association Journal*, 63, 402–405.

Markowe, H. (1988) The frequency of child sexual abuse in the United Kingdom. *Health Trends*, 20, 2–6.

McHugh, S., and Vallis, T. M. (1986) *Illness Behavior: A Multidisciplinary Model*. Plenum, New York.

Meadow, R. (1982) Munchausen syndrome by proxy. *Archives of Disease in Childhood*, 57, 92–98.

Mecham, M., Jex, J., and Jones, J. (1967) *Utah Test of Language Development*. Communication Research Association, Salt Lake City.

Mezzich, J. (1988) On developing a psychiatric multi-axial schema for ICD-10. *British Journal of Psychiatry*, 152 (suppl. 1), 38–43.

Mills, J., and Crowley, R. (1986) *Therapeutic Metaphors for Children and the Child Within*. Brunner Mazel, New York.

Minuchin, S., Rosman, B., and Baker, L. (1978) *Psychosomatic Families: Anorexia Nervosa in Context*. Harvard University Press, Cambridge, Massachusetts.

Monaghan, J., Robinson, J., and Dodge, J. (1979) The Children's Life Events Inventory. *Journal of Psychosomatic Research*, 23, 63–68.

Mrazek, P., and Kempe, C. (1981) *Sexually Abused Children and Their Families*. Pergamon Press, Oxford.

Mrazek, D., and Mrazek, P. (1985) Child maltreatment. In: M. Rutter and L. Hersov (eds), *Child and Adolescent Psychiatry: Modern Approaches* (2nd edn). Blackwell, Oxford.

Murray, H. (1938) *Explorations in Personality*. Oxford University Press, Oxford.

Naish, J., and Apley, J. (1951) Growing pains: A clinical study of non-arthritic limb pains in children. *Archives of Disease in Childhood*, 26, 134–140.

Neale, M. (1956) *Analysis of Reading Ability*. Macmillan, London.

O'Dell, S. (1974) Training parents in behavior modification: A review. *Psychological Bulletin*, 81, 418–433.

Ollendick, T., and Cerny, J. (1983) *Clinical Behavior Therapy with Children*. Plenum: New York.

Perrin, E., and Gerrity, P. (1981) There's a demon in your belly: Children's understanding of illness. *Pediatrics*, 67, 841–849.

Porter, R. (1984) *Sexual Abuse Within the Family*. Tavistock, London.

Reddihough, D., Landau, L., Jones, L., and Richard, W. (1977) Family anxieties in childhood asthma. *Australian Paediatric Journal*, 13, 295–298.

Reynell, J. (1969) *Reynell Developmental Language Scales*. NFER, Windsor.

Rivinus, T., Jamison, D., and Graham, P. (1975) Childhood organic neurological disease presenting as a psychiatric disorder. *Archives of Disease in Childhood*, 50, 115–119.

Rorschach, H. (1942) *Psychodiagnostic: A Diagnostic Test Based on Perception*. Huber, Berne.

Rosse, R. B. (1984) Biopsychosocial 'mapping' with medical students in consultation–liaison psychiatry. *International Journal of Psychiatry in Medicine*, 14, 323–330.

Russell, D. (1983) The incidence and prevalence of intrafamilial and extrafamilial sexual abuse of female children. *Child Abuse and Neglect*, 7, 133–146.

Rutter, M., and Cox, A. (1985) Other family influences. In: M. Rutter and L. Hersov (eds), *Child and Adolescent Psychiatry: Modern Approaches*. Blackwell, Oxford.

Rutter, M., and Gould, M. (1985) Classification. In: M. Rutter and L. Hersov (eds), *Child and Adolescent Psychiatry: Modern Approaches*. Blackwell, Oxford.

Rutter, M., Tizard, J., and Whitmore, K. (1970) *Education, Health and Behaviour*. Longman, London.

Rutter, M., Shaffer, D., and Stage, C. (1975) *A Guide to a Multi-axial Classification Scheme for Child Psychiatric Disorders in Childhood and Adolescence*. Institute of Psychiatry, London.

Satir, V. M. (1978) *Conjoint Family Therapy: A Guide to Theory and Technique*. Science and Behavior Books, Palo Alto, California; Souvenir Press, London.

Schachar, R., Rutter, M., and Smith, A. (1981) The characteristics of situationally and pervasively hyperactive children: Implications for syndrome definition. *Journal of Child Psychology and Psychiatry*, 22, 375–392.

Schonell, F. J., and Schonell, F. E. (1958) *Diagnostic and Attainment Testing*. Oliver & Boyd, Edinburgh.

Shaffer, D., and Ambrosini, P. (1985) Enuresis and sleep disorders. In: J. M. Wiener (ed.), *Diagnosis and Psychopharmacology of Childhood and Adolescent Disorders*. Wiley, Chichester.

Shapiro, E., and Shapiro, A. K. (1981) Tic disorders. *Journal of the American Medical Association*, 245, 1583–1585.

Sifneos, P. (1973) The prevalence of alexithymic characteristics in psychosomatic patients. *Psychotherapy and Psychosomatics*, 22, 255–262.

Skuse, D. (1985) Non-organic failure to thrive: A re-appraisal. *Archives of Disease in Childhood*, 60, 173–178.

Smirnoff, V. (1971) *The Scope of Child Analysis*. Routledge & Kegan Paul, London.

Smith, M., Delves, T., Lansdown, R., Clayton, B., and Graham, P. (1983) The effects of lead exposure on urban children. *Developmental Medicine and Child Neurology*, Suppl 47.

Smithells, R. (1982) In praise of outpatients: Partnership in paediatrics. In: J. Apley and C. Ounstead (eds), *One Child*. Spastics International Medical Publications, London; Lippincott, Philadelphia.

Stapeldon, O. (1932) *Lost Men in London*. Methuen, London.

Steig, W. (1971) *Amos & Boris*. Farrar, Straus & Giroux, New York.

Stuart, R. B. (1982) *Adherence, Compliance and Generalization in Behavioral Medicine*. Brunner-Mazel, New York.

Stutsman, R. (1948) *Guide for Administering the Merrill–Palmer Scale of Mental Tests*. Harcourt, Brace, New York.

Taylor, E. (1986) *The Overactive Child*. Lippincott, Philadelphia; MacKeith Press, London.

Thomas, A., Chess, S., and Birch, H. (1968) *Temperament and Behavior Disorders in Children*. New York University Press, New York.

Thomson, A., and Sills, J. (1988) Diagnosis of functional illness presenting with gait disorder. *Archives of Disease in Childhood*, 63, 148–153.

Thrower, S., Bruce, W., and Walton, F. (1982) The family circle method for integrating family systems concepts in family medicine. *Journal of Family Practice*, 15, 451–457.

Tomson, P. (1983) Family therapy. *Medicine in Practice*, 1, 649–655.

Totman, R. (1979) *Social Causes of Illness*. Pantheon, New York; Souvenir Press, London.

Truax, C., and Carkhuff, R. (1967) *Toward Effective Counseling and Psychotherapy: Training and Practice*. Aldine, Chicago.

Wald, A., Chandra, R., Fisher, S., Gartner, J., and Zitelli, B. (1982) Lactose malabsorption in recurrent abdominal pain of childhood. *Journal of Paediatrics*, **100**, 65–68.

Wallerstein, J. (1983) Children of divorce: Stress and developmental tasks. In: N. Garmezy and M. Rutter (eds), *Stress, Coping and Development in Children*. McGraw-Hill, New York.

Warner, J. O. and Hathaway, M. J. (1984) Allergic form of Meadow's syndrome (Munchausen by proxy). *Archives of Disease in Childhood*, **59**, 151–156.

Wechsler, D. (1976) *Manual for the Wechsler Intelligence Scale for Children: Revised*. NFER, Windsor; Psychological Corporation, New York.

Winefield, H., and Reay, M. (1980) *Behavioural Science in Medicine*. Allen & Unwin, London; University Park Press, Baltimore.

Winnicott, D. W. (1971) *Therapeutic Consultations in Child Psychiatry*. Hogarth Press, London; Basic Books, New York.

Wolff, O. (1986) *Listening to and Talking with Children and Their Parents: Some Lessons Learnt by a Paediatrician*. Hugh Greenwood Lecture, 1986, University of Exeter.

Yamamoto, K., Soliman, A., Parsons, J., and Davis, O. (1987) Voices in unison: Stressful events in the lives of children in six countries. *Journal of Child Psychology and Psychiatry*, **28**, 855–864.

Yeaworth, R., York, J., Hussey, M., Lugle, M., and Goodwin, T. (1980) The development of an adolescent life change event scale. *Adolescence*, **15**, 91–97.

Yule, W. (1985) Behavioural approaches. In: M. Rutter and L. Hersov (eds), *Child and Adolescent Psychiatry: Modern Approaches*. Blackwell, Oxford.

Index

151

WITHDRAWN
FROM STOCK
QMUL LIBRARY